CACTI AND SUCCULENTS
HANDBOOK

CACTI AND
SUCCULENTS
HANDBOOK

Basic Growing Techniques and a Directory of
More Than 140 Common Species and Varieties

GIDEON F. SMITH

COMPANIONHOUSE™
BOOKS

Cacti and Succulents Handbook

CompanionHouse Books™ is an imprint of Fox Chapel Publishers International Ltd.

Project Team
Vice President–Content: Christopher Reggio
Editor: Jeremy Hauck
Copy Editor: Laura Taylor
Design: David Fisk
Index: Jay Kreider

ISBN 978-1-62008-278-2

Library of Congress Cataloging-in-Publication Data

Names: Smith, Gideon, 1959- author.
Title: Cacti and succulents handbook / Gideon F. Smith.
Description: Mount Joy, PA : CompanionHouse Books, 2018. | Includes index.
Identifiers: LCCN 2017058386 | ISBN 9781620082782 (pbk.)
Subjects: LCSH: Cactus. | Succulent plants.
Classification: LCC SB438 .S652 2018 | DDC 634/.775--dc23
LC record available at https://lccn.loc.gov/2017058386

Fox Chapel Publishing
903 Square Street
Mount Joy, PA 17552

Fox Chapel Publishers International Ltd.
7 Danefield Road, Selsey (Chichester)
West Sussex PO20 9DA, U.K.

www.facebook.com/companionhousebooks

We are always looking for talented authors. To submit an idea, please send a brief inquiry to acquisitions@foxchapelpublishing.com.

Printed and bound in Singapore
20 19 18   2 4 6 8 10 9 7 5 3 1

CONTENTS

FOREWORD

Most books that deal with succulents from a horticultural point of view deliberately focus on plants suitable for indoor collections (from window sills to greenhouses) in the northern hemisphere—it is a simple fact that the majority of the cactus and succulent plant hobby communities live in those parts of the world. In contrast, the vast majority of succulent plant species hails from essentially frost-free subtropical, tropical, and temperate regions, and growing them in gardens in those areas, or using them for garden and landscape design in suitable climates, should be at least as popular as growing them indoors in adverse climates. While succulents clearly enjoy popularity in public and private collections in milder climates, the literature on how to successfully grow them under garden conditions is surprisingly almost completely nonexistent.

Gideon F. Smith, the author of the present tome, has ventured to fill this gap when he shared his experience and knowledge for an earlier incarnation of this work published back in 2006. His book refreshingly addressed both audiences: those who have to protect their plants from the elements, as well as those who can grow them anywhere out of doors. The need for an updated and expanded edition testifies that the book indeed filled a long-standing void in the literature available in the field. This new and updated edition is thus to be highly welcomed.

But why is it that succulents with their remarkable combination of attractive and simultaneously repulsive characters have developed into cherished and sought-after garden plants? Perhaps it is just this enigmatic mixture as shown by fierce spination, or threateningly toothed leaf margins, in combination with colorful and varied inflorescences and flowers that is responsible for their popularity. In addition, succulents are perfect examples of the wonders of plant survival under sometimes extreme and adverse climatic conditions; remarkably, at the same time, they will readily thrive in a garden, regardless of its shape and size. Even a degree of horticultural neglect—a feature certainly welcomed by busy gardeners—will do them no harm.

Gideon, a professional botanist with a long-standing interest in all aspects of succulent plant biology, is to be congratulated for firstly having written this book, and secondly for updating it in the form of this improved, new edition. He has successfully amalgamated his botanical knowledge with personal horticultural experience, and presents a prime example of how scientists should not keep exclusively to their laboratories, herbaria, and offices, but should step out and bridge the gap between science on the one hand, and popular horticulture and the hobby community on the other hand.

Already Johann Wolfgang Goethe (August 28, 1749–March 22, 1832), the celebrated German author and statesman, was fascinated by a succulent plant, namely what we today know as *Kalanchoe pinnata*, and its capacity to grow new plants from the leaf margins. While exactly this property makes the plant a problematic invasive weed in many places, it is also a good example of how succulents fascinate people around the world. Gideon has endeavored to enhance this fascination, and I am sure that this revised and updated book will again achieve this goal.

Sukkulenten-Sammlung Zürich   **Urs Eggli, PhD**
Zürich, Switzerland
June 13, 2017

PREFACE TO THE NEW EDITION

The first edition of *Cacti and Succulents* was published in 2006 by New Holland Publishers Ltd., and now 11 years later, it is being republished as an second edition by Fox Chapel Publishing. This second edition of *Cacti and Succulents Handbook* features over 100 common, and not-so-common, cacti and succulents. *Cacti and Succulents Handbook* remains an accessible, user-friendly guide to the identification and cultivation of these popular plants. As before, color photographs portray all the species covered, and authoritative text describes key identification and other features. This book will have wide appeal both among naturalists and to the gardening public who want to know more about these fascinating plants.

One of the primary aims of this edition remains to excite succulent plant collectors, gardeners, tourists, and natural historians about the magnificent global succulent flora. To keep the book accessible to a large and diverse interest group, this edition is written in straightforward language that will appeal to amateur collectors and professional botanists alike. Given the popularity of the earlier book, those species treated in that work have been retained in this new edition.

The main purpose of *Cacti and Succulents Handbook* is to familiarize readers with a selection of cacti and succulent species. Special emphasis is placed on the family Cactaceae, the flowering plant group in which all species of cactus are included. In addition, a selection of easy-to-grow succulent species, spread across twelve families, is discussed.

Succulent tissues have been recorded in the leaves, stems, and roots—or a combination of these organs—in about 10,000 plant species globally. These species that often, but not always, occur in regions where rainfall is low or erratic are spread across about 80 flowering plant families. However, even in high-rainfall regions, locally dry sites such as sheer cliff faces or the well-drained forks of tree branches abound; in these positions succulents often also grow in abundance. Succulents occur in most arid, subtropical, Mediterranean, and tropical regions of the world, but perhaps the best known of these are southern Africa, which is host to well over 4,700 such species, and Mexico and the southern United States.

Introductory pages are provided to each of the families dealt with. These introductory texts give some basic information about the families, and illustrate typical representatives as well as some of their characteristic features. The family introductions are followed by the species treatments.

Since this book was first published, a number of developments have taken place in the field of domestic gardening:

- **Planting indigenous has become firmly entrenched.**
- **Water-wise gardening has become very popular.**
- **There is increasing awareness of the sometimes negative impact humans can have on the well-being of the planet.**

Cacti and succulents come in a large variety of shapes and sizes. Some are trees of over 65 ft. (20 m) tall, while others are low-growing soil huggers that look like the rocks and stones among which they grow.

Given the popularity that succulents have attained in horticulture in general, this book will further inspire gardeners who prefer low-maintenance and waterwise plants for cultivation. The variety of succulents available in nursery and plant centers today ranges from large-growing trees suitable for estate and ranch gardens, to tiny ones that will thrive in windowsill pots and hanging baskets.

In this new edition of *Cacti and Succulents Handbook* the cacti and succulents are deliberately discussed under the families in which they are included. Family concepts are well-known and it will be easy to locate plants with similar characteristics.

In recent times research results have contributed to a better understanding of relationships among plants; this has resulted in a rearrangement of groups of species, for example in the Aloe family where several new genera were created, and ones long-disused resurrected. Similarly, for example, the family Portulacaceae has been split into several smaller ones.

I hope you will derive much pleasure from this updated book.

May 2017   **Gideon F. Smith**

Dramatic sculptural shapes like these enhance the stark atmosphere and beauty of this desert landscape.

CULTIVATING CACTI AND SUCCULENTS

Cacti and succulents invoke a response in anyone who lays eyes on them. They are simply too dramatic and diverse for them not to be noticed. They might be stared at in bewilderment, or dismissed as bizarre, but they can never be ignored, for they are fascinating and, to many plant collectors, highly attractive and desirable.

Their magnificent architectural and sculptural shapes will enhance most garden settings. Columnar and treelike types look like sentries standing silent guard outside a house or beside a swimming pool.

Cacti and succulent flowers are exceptionally decorative, even though some tend to be short-lived. Flowering is not just another routine of nature; it is a real event.

The thin, wiry branches of *Fouquiera splendens* and the thick trunk of *Carnegiea gigantea* stand out against the clouds.

WHAT ARE CACTI AND SUCCULENTS?

In cultivation, cacti and succulents generally have globular, columnar, leaflike, or wiry, rosulate, or treelike bodies that are fat and swollen. They are variously adorned with spots, fissures, and ridges and, of course, often rather rapier-like teeth and spines.

In their natural habitats, numerous species alter their appearance with the seasons: from seemingly lifeless at the height of the arid season to exploding with vigorous growth when the rains finally arrive, after which they usually flower, sending forth spectacular large-scale, almost overgrown, clustered or single blooms.

Even when very young, as developing buds, cactus and succulent flowers hold the promise of striking beauty. They take their time to reach maturity then, all of a sudden, they explode into vivid color, often fading within a few days. This is, of course, part of their charisma and contributes to turning each flowering into a real happening.

During the rainy season, cacti and succulents absorb moisture that must last them until the next, often unpredictable, showers arrive. The ridges and grooves of their fluted stems and leaves expand as they absorb life-giving water.

This precious cargo is then slowly and carefully used to sustain the plants through the next dry season (sometimes through multiple dry seasons), until they can once again replenish their water-storage organs.

Thus the cycle continues and the plants keep on surviving in an endlessly arid environment.

Cactus and succulent species differ vastly in shape and size. Some, such as the well-known saguaro or "cowboy cactus" (*Carnegiea gigantea*), or the giant yuccas (*Yucca filifera* and *Yucca aloifolia*) and tree aloes (*Aloidendron barberae* and *Aloidendron dichotomum*), can reach a height of over 65 ft. (20 m), while others are no taller than a few stacked coins.

Some cacti and succulent plant bodies remain underground, exposing only their flowers to pollinators; others take the form of bougainvillea-like scramblers, shrubby trees, climbers with angled stems, spiny, rounded barrels, or are spindly and thin-stemmed with massive, tuber-like underground storage organs—the list is almost endless and offers an embarrassingly rich variety from which to choose plants to cultivate.

This diversity is echoed in the habitats that they occupy. These range from high rainfall tropical rainforests, to some of the hottest and most arid deserts on earth, and from sea level, where they are exposed to desiccating salt spray, to high mountains where they may be seasonally covered by snow.

As horticultural objects to admire, collect, and grow, cacti and succulents find favor among modern city dwellers, regardless of whether they have large, sprawling, landscaped gardens or postage stamp-sized balconies or rooftop gardens with space for a few choice plants only. This popularity can be attributed to a number of factors:

- Most cacti and succulent species tolerate extreme horticultural abuse. Indeed, most species are not precious, princess-like plants requiring undue pampering. Plants will easily stay firm and green, even if somewhat deprived of water and nutrients. Container-grown plants do not require regular repotting, and grow quite happily, even when their roots are pot-bound.
- Most species are not fussy about climate and growing conditions and, with some attention to a few basic rules, will survive as easily indoors as outside. There will always be a selection of species that will thrive in your local conditions, so you don't need to manipulate the micro-climate to have a group of plants to boast about. They require little attention to look their best, which is handy if you don't have much time available for gardening.

- Furthermore, although most species are fairly slow-growing, they will give years of pleasure. This contrasts sharply with garden annuals that often require labor-intensive horticultural care.
- The juice-filled bodies of most cacti and succulents are exceedingly resistant to attacks by pests. If they are subject to insect infestations, these can generally be treated with great ease.

SCIENTIFIC VERSUS COMMON NAMES

Strictly speaking, all plants have a single, unique Latin or Latinized scientific name. This is the ideal situation, but it does not always apply, as some plants are known by different names, often depending on which authority is asked to supply a name for a plant.

At the species rank, a scientific name consists of a combination of a genus name and a specific epithet, which together constitute the species name (e.g. *Yucca filifera*).

Not all species have common names. Although these are often very interesting and descriptive, they tend to be poorly known and are not that widely used. Furthermore, a single species can have many common names, which can create confusion, especially if the names are only of limited regional use.

KINGDOM ▶ DIVISION ▶ CLASS ▶ FAMILY ▶ GENUS ▶ SPECIES

BOTANICAL CLASSIFICATION

Botanical, indeed biological, classification is most commonly done according to a so-called hierarchical system. This means that each higher rank (such as an order or a family) includes a number of subordinate groups that share certain characteristics. A family, for example, consists of one or more genera, each of which has more in common with one another than with genera of other families. With genera it's the same, but they comprise one or more related species, of course.

For collectors of succulent plants, the genus and species ranks tend to be the most important categories, as collectors often become interested in species with a similar appearance and then, once the collecting bug has bitten, expand their collections with similar-looking entities. And, of course, species included in a single genus often exhibit numerous essentially similar characteristics. However, there should be discontinuities among the characters of species as, without them, classification would be impossible. In addition, a reproductive barrier is sometimes encountered between different species. In the plant kingdom, however, this reproductive barrier is usually absent as hybrids between even distantly related species can sometimes be fully fertile. In contrast, interspecific hybrids in the animal kingdom are usually completely infertile.

Defining Cacti

The broadly defined group of about 10,000 water-storing species that is distributed worldwide and which is generally referred to as "succulents" belong to as many as 80 different, often unrelated, plant families. Of these, about 1,800 are species of cactus but, in vivid contrast to the rest of the succulents, all cacti belong to only a single family of flowering plants, the Cactaceae. All cacti are therefore succulent in that they store water in at least one of their organs—the stems, leaves, or roots. (Even the leaves of the bougainvillea-like *Pereskia* species, which are large, flat, and persistent, are somewhat fleshy.)

Fortunately, it is quite easy to distinguish cacti from succulent plants because they have certain characteristics that set them apart from all other plants, including the non-cactoid succulents, some of which, such as the euphorbias, closely resemble cacti, especially from a distance. Although flower characteristics are the most useful indicator when plants are identified, it is not necessary to have flowers available when trying to decide whether one is dealing with species of cactus.

The following, easy-to-observe characteristics make it simple to recognize a cactus, even when it is not in flower.

1. Without exception, cacti are characterized by the presence of small, cushion-like structures on the plant bodies called areoles (seen here as white, furry "spots" on *Parodia horstii*). These are specialized structures from which all cactus growth occurs and include new stem segments (also called pads), flowers, and spines. (The spines of species of the milkweed family, the Euphorbiaceae, do not arise from areoles; a clear indication that the cactus-lookalike euphorbias are not cacti at all.)

2. Representatives of the cactus family, such as this columnar *Pachycereus marginatus*, are mostly, but not exclusively, stem succulents; that is, the inner tissues of their stems serve as storage organs. This indicates clearly that many species are naturally distributed in areas of low rainfall. Cacti that occur in high-rainfall tropical areas are restricted to locally dry sites, such as the well-drained humus pockets accumulating in forked branches of trees or small pockets of soil against cliff faces.

3. The plant bodies of many cactus species, such as the opuntias or prickly pears, consist of leafless flattened stem segments (also referred to as pads, paddles, or joints), depicted here on *Opuntia phaeacantha*, commonly known as the tulip prickly pear. These segments can also be angled, tubular, or leaflike. The pads are various shades of green and have taken over photosynthetic (food-producing) activities performed by the leaves of conventional plants.

4. Most, but not all, cactus species are armed with spines (as here on the ribs of *Pachycereus pringlei*, the Elephant cactus or Mexican giant cardon). These vary tremendously in terms of shape, size, and rigidity, and clear distinctions can be made between the different types of spines carried on the areoles of cacti (that is, whether they are positioned centrally or radially). The spines always serve one or more functions, such as protecting plants from grazing animals, or against excessive solar radiation, or assisting some species with the dispersal of stem segments when they get hooked onto the coats of roving animals.

For the purpose of simplification, no distinction is made in this book between the different types of central or radial spines of cacti.

5. The areoles of some species, such as this *Opuntia microdasys*, are adorned with tufts of small, bristly hairs called glochids. To the layman these miniature structures are only a variation on the theme of "spines" as they can cause immense irritation to exposed skin. The glochids of most species are barbed, like fish hooks or harpoons, and difficult to dislodge once they have become established in one's flesh.

6. In many species of cactus, the flowers are produced from a so-called cephalium. This refers to a densely woolly or bristly "head" which may occur at the apex of a globular cactus or on one side of a columnar cactus. In the latter case, they are usually referred to as lateral or pseudo-cephalia, as seen here on *Cephalocereus columna-trajani*.

7. The bodies and flowers of cacti come in a bewildering diversity of shape, size, and color. However, cactus flowers are generally fairly large and brightly colored, like this *Echinopsis vatteri*, unless the species is night-flowering, in which case its flowers are usually a muted white or creamish color. This, along with the marvelously variable shapes and sizes of their stems contributes significantly to their allure for the collector. The flowers can be broadly regarded as funnel-shaped, starting out thin at their points of attachment to the areoles on the stems, then broadening considerably toward their tips, exposing the reproductive organs (pollen-bearing stamens and receptive stigmas) to animal and insect visitors that effect pollination.

8. Plant shape is a very constant character within a particular species of cactus. However, it is not uncommon to find vastly divergent body shapes in a particular genus. The architecture of cactus plant bodies, which results in their definitive shapes, can be divided into a number of very distinct types that facilitate plant identification.

IDENTIFYING CACTI PLANT SHAPES

Mammillaria muehlenpfordtii

Globular or **spherical cacti** with small to medium-sized, globular to spherically rounded plant bodies are the most popular among collectors, especially those with only limited space for a few pots. Many species with this growth-form remain solitary, while others tend to sprout offshoots from the base, resulting in anything from small to large clumps of very attractive cushion-shaped plants.

Stenocereus thurberi

Harrisia martinii

Climbing cacti. Species of cactus belonging to this group have comparatively weak, ropelike stems that will rapidly climb onto any nearby supporting structure.

Columnar. These species tend to be large-growing, with their stems often reaching a height of several meters. Some species produce single stems or "columns," while others branch from the base, or higher up the stem, to produce sparse to dense candelabra-like clumps, with a rather bushy collection of cactus stems.

Hanging cacti. Hanging cacti have either thin, pencil-, or ropelike stems, or fairly broad leaflike, sometimes flattened stems, which invariably dangle downward as they cannot support themselves. They generally make perfect subjects for cultivation in hanging baskets.

Schlumbergera truncata

DEFINING SUCCULENTS

To even attempt to provide a list of defining characteristics for succulents would be futile, short of stating that they do not have areoles, as cacti do. Succulents are simply too diverse and distributed among too many families to define them in a few paragraphs. The approach followed here is to briefly mention a selection of some of the more easily recognizable characteristics of the families that include succulents where their representatives are discussed in the book.

An *Echeveria* in flower clings tenaciously to its rocky home. Informal plantings like this can add interest to a garden.

A majestic saguaro, the typical "cowboy cactus" (*Carnegiea gigantea*), stands sentinel against a looming desert storm.

CACTI AND SUCCULENT DISTRIBUTION

Cacti and succulents are well-adapted to an arid life, having developed a host of water-saving mechanisms in order to survive. However, "arid areas" should not only be equated to deserts. Contrary to popular belief, extreme desert areas are not rich in cactus species. By far the largest number of cacti occur in dry, savanna-like areas where they evade the scorching sun by seeking out the protection provided by associated shrubs or grasses.

WHERE ARE CACTI FOUND?

In their geographical distribution, cacti are more or less restricted to the Americas. Only a single subspecies, *mauritiana*, of a variable species of hanging forest cactus, *Rhipsalis baccifera*, occurs widely in Africa, with this and other subspecies of the same species inhabiting the islands of Madagascar and Sri Lanka in the Indian Ocean.

The largest diversity of cacti occurs in Mexico and the southern USA, but significant numbers come from northern Argentina, southern Bolivia, Peru, Brazil, and Paraguay. In these countries,

cacti are not restricted to arid desert-like parts only. They also occur in extremely cold climates, with some even tolerating the low winter temperatures of the East Coast of the USA. Still other species grow on some of the highest mountain ranges of South America.

Surprisingly, a significant number of cacti species are native to humid tropical rainforests, while other species are found along the Pacific coastlines of Mexico and California, where they are subjected to salt spray and fog drifting in from the ocean.

Given these widely divergent natural habitats of cacti, plus the phenomenal resilience of most species from a horticultural point of view, there are species suitable for cultivation in almost any environment and location, from a small windowsill collection to a large, natural outdoor xerophytic (cactus-strewn) landscape.

Where are succulents found?

Succulents occur on all the continents, with the exception of the poles. They have a vast distribution range and inhabit both hemispheres, from northern continental Europe southward to Australia, and even to some of New Zealand's islands.

Admittedly, at their northern and southern extremes, succulent diversity is low, with the majority of species concentrated much closer to the equator.

The highest natural concentration of succulents is in South Africa, where an astonishing 47 percent-plus of all the world's succulents occur in an area that amounts to less than 10 percent of the global land surface.

Mexico and the southern United States are also home to large numbers of succulents.

How do cactus plants survive?

By reducing, virtually to zero, the amount of leaf surface exposed to an arid, desiccating atmosphere, cacti avoid losing moisture via their leaf stomata (microscopic "breathing" apertures on the leaves of most plants, that allow them to partially regulate their temperatures through evaporative cooling).

Unlike cacti, many species of succulent plants do have leaves. In certain cases, such as the aloes and agaves, the leaves are thick and fleshy, and accumulate large quantities of water when it rains. The leaves then remain fat and turgid for long periods, as the moisture is slowly released to maintain essential physiological processes in the plant's body–until the next downpour starts the process all over again.

Two succulent species, *Euphorbia ledienii* var. *ledienii* (foreground) and *Aloe ferox* (background), growing together in the Eastern Cape, South Africa.

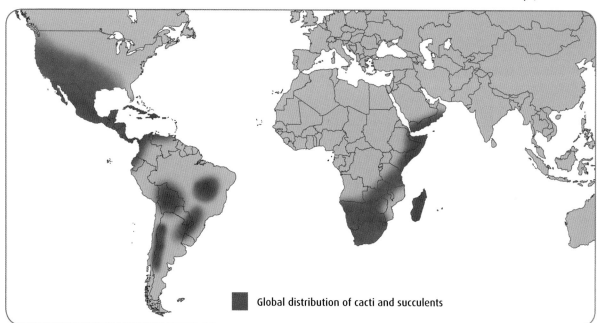

Global distribution of cacti and succulents

The broad natural geographical dispersion of cactus and succulent species is depicted on the map, although some species may occur outside these areas. Cultivated plants can be found throughout the world, provided the growing conditions are suitable.

Small-growing species of cactus, such as *Mammillaria pennispinosa*, will even flower in a seedling tray.

CULTIVATING CACTI AND SUCCULENTS

Cactus plants are some of the most desirable species to cultivate as they are so tolerant of a variety of different growing conditions. Most species, regardless of their climatic preferences, thrive both indoors and outdoors, and most flower annually.

Many cactus species can be grown from cuttings that root easily, making it possible to quickly obtain large plants that will proliferate and flower. Apart from being grown in open garden beds, a wide selection of species is also suitable for long-term container gardening, requiring comparatively little aftercare once they become established in pots.

There are almost as many opinions about the successful cultivation of cacti as there are collectors of these plants. Some species are more difficult to grow than others, but the following guidelines should work for most species.

SELECTING THE RIGHT PLANT

Although young cacti are available from nurseries and specialist growers, part of the challenge is to grow your own from scratch. Cultivating plants is not for everyone, as it takes time and dedication but, for an avid gardener, it offers many rewards. The first step is to select the "parents" of your future cacti.

TAKING CUTTINGS

A cutting is essentially a section of a larger plant that is identical in genetic composition to the plant from which it has been removed. Cuttings range in size and length from a little globule only a few millimeters long to ones that can be quite large and several centimeters in length. "Cuttings" longer than 3 ft. (1 m) are sometimes called truncheons.

The cacti and succulent species that are best suited to propagation from cuttings are typically those that grow as branched shrubs or produce basal sprouts. Conversely, if the species you want to propagate remain as single-bodied, unbranched specimens for the duration of their life cycles, you may not have any other option but to raise the next generation from seed.

Cuttings should, ideally, be taken from healthy, strongly growing plants. As a rule of thumb, propagation is best at the onset of the growing season (that is, in spring for summer growers and in autumn for winter growers). However, many experienced growers claim that, short of a few hard-to-grow species, propagation of most cacti and succulents can be attempted throughout the year, especially in mild climates.

However, if you are in doubt about the possible

success of your propagation efforts, or fear that you may end up with a badly mutilated, highly prized specimen and no rooted cuttings to show for it, then wait for the onset of the next growing season. Otherwise, if availability of material is not a problem, give it a try at any time of the year.

Generally speaking, it is safest to attempt propagation from pieces of a parent plant that have attained a reasonable degree of maturity. It is much easier to lose material if it is of insufficient girth and/or length. Remember, the cutting has to sustain itself for a few days, weeks, or even months on accumulated water and nutrition reserves, before it produces its own roots.

Although many species are not too fussy when it comes to the medium used for rooting cuttings, a mixture consisting of equal parts of gritty sand and sifted potting mix generally works well for many cacti and succulents.

Freshly planted cuttings should be given some protection against severe sunlight, at least until the cutting has rooted. The soil mixture should be kept moist, not wet throughout. However, cuttings generally do not need to be fed. At this early stage in the life of a new, rooted plant, emphasis is on its survival (i.e., striking root), rather than on producing fat, new growth.

The newly rooted material can be kept in the rooting mixture for a long time, provided the size of the container used conforms to that of the cutting.

However, if you deliberately used a very small saucer or seedling tray in which to root cuttings, the plant material can be transplanted as soon as it shows signs of active growth.

The cuttings will usually show new growth within a matter of weeks (even days, in the case of some species).

How to take a cutting

Use a sharp knife or pair of pruners (secateurs) to remove a section of the cactus plant body, preferably at the point where the stem segments (pads) join together.

This is usually the thinnest part of the cactus stem and, in most species, it is quite easy to cut through the joints. (In the case of suckering species, or globular ones that proliferate through forming small plantlets, the suckers or miniature plants should be removed carefully with a sharp knife, as close to the main stem as possible.)

Leave the removed parts in a shady position for a few days, to allow them to dry before they are planted.

To root these cuttings, dip them into commercially available rooting hormone powder and insert them into a friable, well drained soil mixture containing coarse (sharp) sand or gravel (grit).

The length to which a cutting should be inserted into the soil depends on the size and length of the cutting. Generally,

To take a cutting, use pruners (secateurs) or a sharp knife to remove a section of the cactus plant.

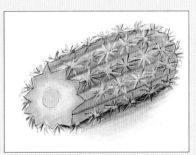

To root cuttings, dip them into rooting hormone powder.

Insert the cutting into the soil at sufficient depth to allow it to take.

a good insertion length for a small to medium-size cutting is one that will allow the rootless plant material to remain erect in the soil mixture. Large cuttings should be staked to provide support and prevent them from toppling over.

SOWING SEEDS

Cacti seeds are generally borne in the juice-laden, fleshy fruit. The best germination results are usually obtained from seeds that are freshly collected as soon as the fruits are ripe and burst open.

To prepare the seeds for sowing, the sugary pulp in which they are embedded should be removed. Seeds can be manually picked out of the sugary pulp, or the pulp can be washed off with water, and the seeds left to dry. Once they are dry, wash the seeds with a weak solution of household bleach, and leave them to dry again, before sowing.

Sow the seeds sparingly in large, flat seed trays that have been filled with a soil mixture consisting of one-third coarse (sharp) river sand (ideally not quarried sand, which is too fine), one-third well-rotted and sieved compost, and one-third garden soil.

To promote germination, seedling trays should be provided with adequate air circulation, reasonable warmth, and high humidity.

Ventilation is particularly important once the first seedlings appear, as it promotes the cyclic drying out of the soil, but take care that the soil never becomes bone-dry, as this could kill the seedlings. To keep the soil in a seedling tray moist, but not wet, stand the tray in a larger container of water and remove it as soon as water appears on the soil surface. Seedlings have very poor root systems, and watering them from below also prevents the seedlings from being washed out of the soil by a careless jet of water. Young seedlings generally don't need additional feeding, as the sifted compost mixture contains all the required nutrients.

High humidity can be created by inserting a seed tray into a transparent plastic bag and closing it with a piece of thin wire. To prevent fungal spores from ruining newly germinated seedlings, add a commercially available fungicide to the first watering of the tray, before placing it in the bag.

Once the seedlings are about the size of an adult man's pinky fingernail, they can be removed from the seedling tray and potted into small, individual pots. Although they can be potted out when smaller, the risk of losing them is much greater, as their root systems are very small and fragile at this early stage of their development.

Germinating temperatures

A temperature of between 59°F and 77°F (15°C and 25°C) is ideal for germinating cactus seeds. Temperatures that drop below or rise above these levels can delay germination or halt it altogether.

Plants of *Echinocactus grusonii* (yellow, ball-shaped plants in the foreground) and *Pachycereus pringlei* (green, columnar plants in the middle ground) have been planted out into raised beds.

OTHER METHODS OF CULTIVATION

When the pads of some species, especially opuntias, are simply severed and left on the ground, they will spontaneously root and form small plants at some of the areoles.

Other species, especially tree-dwelling epiphytic cacti, such as species of *Schlumbergera*, will form aerial roots that facilitate the formation of a healthy rootstock once they have been removed from the mother plant and planted in the desired spot or container.

Advanced growers may attempt to graft the more difficult-to-grow species onto rootstock plants that grow easily. The challenge is to ensure that the vascular (transport) tissue of the material is aligned and that the two plants are securely attached to one another. This takes some practice and beginners should not be surprised if their early grafting efforts fail.

Commercially available seed

Packets of seed for cacti and succulents can occasionally be found at nurseries and garden centers. These seeds have usually been washed and dried and can be sown directly into seedling trays.

Special nurseries or horticultural societies sometimes offer seed that can be ordered from their annually distributed seed catalogs. These can be sown upon receipt.

Deadheading

This is the process through which the fading flowers of a perennial shrub or annual herb are removed to prevent the formation of fruit and seed. Seed production is a high-energy process, so plants in this stage of their life cycle are unlikely to produce more flowers. However, if the spent flowers are pinched out (deadheaded), many plants will be stimulated to produce a second crop of flowers.

Not many cacti or succulent species require deadheading, but some companion plants, such as the profusely flowering daisy shrubs (including the white-purple flowered *Dimorphotheca fruticosa* of which the first crop of flowers are fading), may be enticed into another burst of color if they are given this treatment in midsummer.

HANDLING CACTI

Handling ferociously spined cactus plants, especially medium- to large-size ones, can be tricky.

When planting or transplanting, an easy method is to wrap thick layers of newspaper around the plants before moving them. Another option is to wear heavy protective gloves that will not be readily pierced by the spines.

Spring-loaded wooden tongs (of the type used for turning barbecued meat) can be useful when handling smaller cactus specimens.

The easiest way of propagating *Echinopsis huascha* is by taking stem cuttings that will root very rapidly and soon give rise to identical plants. The reddish orange flowering form is depicted here.

It will take a bit of experimentation to find the right combination of light, water, and nutrients to have healthy plants, but the wait is always worthwhile. For this specimen of *Ferocactus wislizeni* subsp. *herrerae,* the perfect balance has been found.

CARING FOR CACTI AND SUCCULENTS

All plants, including cacti and succulents, have three basic requirements to ensure healthy growth: water, light, and nutrients. Successful cultivation of these fat-bodied plants depends on knowing how these three requirements should be regulated.

Healthy, well-cared-for cacti provide the grower with years of pleasure, but at least as many plants die from under-watering and inadequate nourishment as from overwatering and excessive feeding. Cacti are truly tough plants, although they do require attention if you want keep and develop a desirable and flourishing collection.

When it comes to gardening, cacti and succulents cater to individuals with a wide range of needs and skills, from those with not-so-green thumbs to gardeners and horticulturists who thrive on the challenge of bringing hard-to-grow species to flowering maturity.

To achieve success with growing cacti, remember the following:

* Give plants too little water rather than too much.
* Bright light rather than deep shade is best.
* Give sufficient fertilizer, especially when the plants are in flower.

WATER

Although it is not difficult to master the art of watering cacti, it requires some experimentation and careful observation. The golden rule should be "less is more"; that is, err on the low side until you are accustomed to your plants' needs. They may suffer from water stress at first, but you are less likely to lose them.

Watering outdoor plants

While most cacti and succulents can survive on comparatively little water, if you want them to flourish, they should receive adequate water. This is especially true if you want healthy plants, even in times of drought.

Water should not be withheld during the growing and flowering seasons, when plants actively recycle organic carboniferous material and inorganic nutrients as part of the process of increasing their body mass, and accumulate resources to eventually produce their magnificent blooms.

However, once a plant begins to enter its resting phase, which could be in winter or summer, depending on the species, it is usually advisable to limit watering to the occasional spraying.

Plants grown in open beds obtain their water mainly from rainfall. If this is insufficient, then additional irrigation should be provided from time to time to enable them to absorb a sufficient amount of water.

Fortunately, many cactus and succulent species have a means of demonstrating when they need water: their ribbed stems contract like the fins of a concertina, or their leaves become flat. When these plant organs contract, it is a sure sign that the plant is in dire need of water. But do not wait for the first signs of stress before you give water.

Plants that always suffer from water stress (cacti with ribs closely packed rather than expanded), are more prone to succumb to attacks from a variety of pests. To keep your plants healthy, do not allow them to go without water.

Cacti and succulents do not like "cold, wet feet," meaning they prefer not to spend long periods in cold, water-logged soil. This is less of a concern if the plants are grown in open beds or unsheltered spots where water rapidly drains away or the sun naturally dries out the soil. Plants grown in such positions are less prone to rotting, even if at times they receive too much rain from unseasonably high downpours.

Watering indoor plants

Container plants kept indoors or away from the direct effects of the elements depend on the gardener to regulate their watering regimes wisely. One way of doing this is to grow your plants in soil mixtures that retain moisture to varying degrees. For example, if you have a heavy hand with the watering can or hose, make sure that the soil mixture is friable and open, making for good drainage.

Another way to regulate soil moisture in containers is to grow cacti in different types of pots. Plastic pots are popular and affordable but they tend not to breathe, and therefore retain water. On the other hand, clay and ceramic pots lose water through evaporation, so plants grown in them should be watered more frequently than those in plastic containers.

Ideally, potted plants should be watered in the morning, to allow the foliage to dry off before nightfall (this is particularly relevant when nighttime temperatures are low).

In a cold climate, it can be detrimental to give container plants, regardless of whether they are kept indoors or in a greenhouse, tap water that is only a few degrees above zero, as the plants may go into shock.

Before watering, make a point of allowing the water to reach room temperature (± 60°F/15°C). This can be done by filling a few buckets or watering cans and leaving them to stand indoors for a few hours before watering the plants.

Although succulents are not overly susceptible to cold-water stress, they will benefit from an application of water that has reached room temperature.

Plants that are kept outdoors are generally more likely to become progressively acclimatized to the cold weather, and therefore also the lower temperatures of the tap water.

With suitable protection against the elements, particularly very low temperatures and excessive rainfall, some cacti, such as *Opuntia humifusa* can be grown outdoors. This specimen is cultivated in climatically severe Zürich, Switzerland, in an open bed.

A *Euphorbia* adds both contrast and sculptural interest to a courtyard.

to answer. If cacti and succulents receive too little light, they will etiolate (become thin and whitened) unnaturally. If they receive too much light, they will become sunburnt. This usually manifests as unsightly spots on the surface, where the tissue was damaged.

Plants that prefer full sun but have been kept in the shade for a while should be acclimatized slowly, otherwise there is a good chance that they will be badly scorched, or even die, as a result. Remember that even though cacti and succulents grow in desert conditions, they often survive in the shade of nurse plants where they are protected from the damaging rays of the harsh desert sun.

Although it is difficult to be absolute, cacti species with prominent spines generally need high levels of sunlight to retain their shapes and sizes. Species with flattened, leaflike stems require good, but filtered, light. This can be done very easily at home by growing these plants in dappled shade or on a patio in full shade.

Nutrients

Most plants obtain the life-giving inorganic nutrients necessary to sustain growth and development from the medium in which they grow.

This also applies to cacti, even those that grow in very small rock crevices or as epiphytes in the forks of trees. In both cases, nutrients are obtained from the small amount of windblown soil or organic leaf-litter that accumulates over the years in these microhabitats.

In open garden beds, plants benefit from a regular inflow of nutrients as part of the normal cycle of life. But, even so, it is occasionally necessary to dig decaying organic matter (compost) into the ground to replenish depleted nutrient sources. Plants that are regularly fed in this way stay healthy and are far less prone to fall victim to insect infestations and other detrimental pests and diseases.

Although special feeds are sometimes offered for cacti and succulents, most species tend to respond well to commercially available plant feeds. Liquid and foliar feeds are easy to apply and work very well.

Feeding is usually done at the onset of a species' growing season, and regularly (monthly) thereafter, up to the end of the growing season for that species.

Summer and winter watering

There is no simple recipe for advising on the right amount, or frequency, of watering, as there are so many environmental and other factors that determine a plant's needs. This includes the climate, type of soil, ambient air temperature, and local wind conditions.

However, bear in mind that, regardless of any other preference of the species for summer or winter rainfall, neither cacti nor succulents appreciate standing in wet ground, where soil moisture does not drain away.

Light

If it is difficult to advise on the exact watering needs of your plants then, by comparison, the question of exact light conditions is much easier

CACTI and SUCCULENTS HANDBOOK

SEASONAL GARDENING CALENDAR

Once established, most cacti and succulents require very little aftercare and maintenance, other than the normal tasks required by horticulturally tolerant plants. Some seasonal gardening hints and suggestions are given below, but the priority tasks will naturally differ according to where you live and what sort of plants you have, and whether they are grown outdoors all year round, or spend all or part of the year indoors, either in a hothouse or in some other form of shelter.

The division of the gardening year into seasons depends on the climate in your area. If you are a new gardener, a good tip is use a notebook to record what you do, from planting, to pruning, weeding, feeding, and how often you water. By including day-to-day details, such as the rainfall or whether it was sunny or overcast, you will soon build up an invaluable "personal almanac" to refer to year after year.

First month of high summer

High summer does not mean the planting season is over. If planted now, most cacti and succulent species will still root quickly enough to ensure they can withstand the cold winter months.

- Cut back *Pelargonium* species (for example, *Pelargonium peltatum*), that have completed their first flowering of the season. This does not apply to the usually leafless, succulent-stemmed *Pelargonium tetragonum*, for which pruning should hardly be required.
- Plant out *Portulaca* seedlings now, but be sure to provide them with initial protection against the midday sun, and water them regularly. This species does well if you require small plants to grow in the crevices between paving bricks.
- Frangipani trees are now in flower.
- For patient gardeners who planted *Agave wercklei* about eight years ago, the long wait is finally over. In midsummer, this magnificent species produces a towering inflorescence at least 13 ft. (4 m) tall. The upper parts of the flowering pole, or stalk, of this non-suckering species are covered in large clusters of bright yellow flowers.

Second month of high summer

The weather is still very warm and most plants will benefit from an occasional, thorough drenching, ideally with collected rainwater. If you live in a summer rainfall region, make sure the soil is well mulched, especially around shrubs and trees, to promote the absorption and retention of moisture.

- *Portulaca* cultivars perform well and will provide some color, regardless of whether your garden combines various plants with succulents, or is a near-exclusive succulent one.
- The very drought-tolerant, bottle-trunked Australian flame tree, *Brachychiton acerifolius*, now produces spectacular masses of crimson red flowers.

If the climate is right, cacti can be left outdoors all year round, either in open beds or in containers, but in colder climates they may require protection in winter.

First month of late summer

The late summer days are often still exceptionally warm; in some areas, the temperatures are only peaking, and winter rainfall areas are now usually quite dry. Slowly but surely, it is time to say goodbye to summer, at least in terms of planning for the year ahead, and start preparing your garden for autumn and winter, even for spring.

- Do not feed established, summer-growing succulents and non-succulents if your area experiences very cold winters. Feeding will stimulate new growth, which will be destroyed by the first frosts. It is too early to awaken winter-growing succulents from their required and essential summer slumber.
- If the summer rains were good, then thin out and prune climbers, such as the cactus *Quiabentia verticillata*, that have become overgrown. Stake, trim, or tie down creepers (such as the succulent-leaved canary creeper *Senecio tamoides*) that have grown too vigorously during the high summer.
- Plants looking very good at this time of year include frangipani (*Plumeria* species and cultivars) and portulaca (*Portulaca grandiflora* cultivars).

Second month of late summer

- Remove the spent inflorescences of summer-flowering succulents, unless you want to collect the seed.
- **Pests:** Be on the lookout for red spider mite infestations, especially on species of aloe. This pest comes out in force in warm and dry conditions and, in summer rainfall areas, plants produce softer growth, making them highly susceptible to attack. Spray infested plants with a commercially available miticide.

First month of autumn

As days get shorter and temperatures begin to drop, plant growth is noticeably slowing down. Now is the time for a garden cleanup as leaves begin to change color and are shed.

- Stop feeding container plants and give them less water.
- Cut back the succulent-leaved *Plectranthus neochilus* (poor man's lavender), if flowering is finished, but flowers need not be removed. It will resprout quickly.
- Deadhead (pinch out) the first buds of annuals to stimulate them to become more bushy and produce more flowers.

Frangipani (*Plumeria* species and cultivars) comes into flower in late summer.

Second month of autumn

The nights are now getting distinctly chilly, but the days can still be quite pleasant. Autumn is well and truly with us, but it is not yet fully winter.

- Protect plants that are not cold hardy by wrapping them in skirts of long-lasting organic material, such as grass culm wigwams.
- Mulch, mulch, mulch those spent summer flower beds.
- Rake up fallen leaves and put them into a compost bin. Leaf mold takes considerably longer to prepare than compost, but within about 10–12 months the decayed leaves will yield an excellent mulch for spreading out on beds.
- Some early-flowering poinsettias, *Euphorbia pulcherrima*, are coming into bloom.

First month of winter

This time of year signals a period of rest for many plants, but gardeners should start planning now for spring and summer.

- Winter is a good time to clean the leaves of succulents kept indoors. Use tepid or lukewarm water and a very soft rag to wipe off dust and grime, making sure that both the upper and lower leaf surfaces are cleaned. Do not use a brush, as this can damage the natural, often waxy, coating of succulent plant surfaces.
- A multitude of aloe species is now coming into bloom, sending their spectacularly colorful candles skyward.

Second month of winter

In many areas, the temperatures are now even lower than in the previous month, so do not be tempted to remove any protective wrapping from the plants, even if temperatures rise somewhat on the occasional sunny day.

- Do not prune shrubs that have been damaged by frost, as this may stimulate the development of tender new growth that will certainly be affected by the ongoing low temperatures.
- Lightly prune scrambling plants that flowered during late summer and autumn. This group includes *Senecio tamoides* (canary creeper).
- In a summer rainfall region, containers need regular watering (unless you are growing succulents in them).
- This a good time to apply foliar feed to potted plants, especially during dry spells.
- This is the best time for transplanting trees and shrubs if you live in a winter rainfall region.
- Aphids often attack the undersides of leaves of aloes and other succulents at this time of year. Keep a lookout for them and wipe or wash them off.
- Many aloes, such as *Aloe mutabilis* and *Aloe wickensii* var. *wickensii*, are still in full bloom, and garden birds will be feeding on the copious amounts of nectar they produce.

Although it is a summer rainfall species, Aloe marlothii grows quite happily in a dry rock wall in the Kirstenbosch National Botanical Garden, Cape Town, which is situated in a winter rainfall region.

Late winter

Daytime temperatures are now rising, and the first hint of spring is in the air.

- A multitude of different weeds will slowly begin to make their appearance. Remember that ten minutes of weeding daily is much better than having a garden overrun with weeds.

- As the weather warms up, you can start lifting protection from sensitive plants. However, bear in mind that the cold weather may not be over yet.

- Trim poinsettias down to near ground level. Although some people argue that this deforms the plants, they will sprout with renewed vigor in spring and early summer.

Early spring

Spring is definitely in the air and to many people this is the most beautiful month, as new life returns to the garden after the cold, quiet winter months. Existing plants can now be moved and new ones established. This is also the time to plan and prepare for the color you want to display in your summer garden. In preparing for the next few months, the key concepts will be mulch, fertilize, and water wisely.

- Pour liquid fertilizer over your container plants.

- Remove the spent inflorescences of aloe species that bloomed during winter, unless you want to keep their seeds. Cut the side branches into smaller pieces and put them on the compost heap. Allow the short, remaining stumps to dry naturally on the plants, after which they can be easily removed from the rosettes without damaging the crowns. Keep all the twigs, branches, and leaves that are now removed from or shed by your plants for the compost heap.

- Weeds will arrive with the milder weather; eradicate them before they flower and set seed.

- A multitude of insects and garden pests will be attracted by the soft spring growth produced by most plants, including succulents. These insect populations also attract beneficial insects and birds into your garden, so resist the urge to spray your plants with insecticides: you will kill all the animals that feed in your urban paradise.

- Stake fragile plants, such as the canary creeper, if your area is subject to spring winds. Dry, desiccating winds make plants look ragged and unkempt, so trim them as necessary.

- This is a good time of year to take cuttings, which should be planted in a mixture of coarse river sand and sifted compost.

- The Red Texan (*Hesperaloe parviflora*), with its long, gracefully curved inflorescences, looks particularly good at this time of year, and a multitude of mesembs, such as *Oscularia deltoides* with its deep pink flowers, are coming into bloom.

Nectar-loving birds will relish the opportunity to feast on the inflorescences of various aloe species, such as *Aloe arborescens*, when they come into bloom.

Late spring

Temperatures are now consistently higher than over the past few months. This invariably means that your garden will require more maintenance, as weeds establish themselves more easily.

- Inspect your hanging baskets. Repair the netting, add fresh soil if needed, and fertilize them with a liquid fertilizer.
- Sow the fine, almost dust-like seed of the succulent-leaved portulaca cultivars (selections and hybrids of *Portulaca grandiflora*), as they will produce an astonishingly variable riot of color in your garden in a few months time. Many mesembs, such as *Lampranthus amoenus*, are still ablaze with color.

Early summer

The early summer months are usually delightfully warm and one of the best times to simply sit back and enjoy your hard labor over the past 12 months.

- Water containers more frequently, as they tend to dry out faster than open beds exposed to summer rainfall. Hot, desiccating winds will quickly dry out the soil in traditional winter rainfall areas. Beds with non-succulent companion plants, especially those with shallow root systems, must be watered well.
- A number of mesembs, including the excellent ground cover *Aptenia cordifolia*, are still flowering in open garden beds, especially if the soil has been adequately prepared and mulched.
- If *Aloiampelos tenuior*, the scrambling aloe, is grown in well-mulched soil and watered regularly, it will produce lots of inflorescences.

Regular weeding and plant maintenance is required if you want your cacti and succulent beds to reflect your love of these plants. *Kalanchoe luciae*, with its soup plate-sized leaves flowers at the center of this planting. The rosulate, blue-leaved *Agave pumila* grows in the foreground.

Potted cacti can be grouped together to create an area of interest, and it is easy to vary the display by adding or removing plants.

GARDENING AND LANDSCAPING

In most parts of the world, the best seasons for outdoor gardening are autumn and spring. Continental winters are often characterized by heavy drifts of snow, while subtropical areas have long, hot, often humid, summers. The first is not conducive to gardening and the second not to gardeners. This easily becomes apparent when one starts jotting down observations on succulent plant collections and gardens, their creators, and gardening trends.

For avid and enthusiastic collectors of cacti and succulents, indeed for enthusiastic gardeners in general, there is no such thing as an aimless ramble in the countryside or a pointless suburban walk. Throughout, one tends to take notes, both mental and written, while contemplating how to transform one's urban landscape into a personalized piece of succulent paradise.

The best memories, ideas, or reflections often come during chance meetings or unexpected situations. Indeed, being somewhere without preconceived ideas, and intentions affords one an easy and pleasant observation of things. Imagine encountering a window box of *Aloe arborescens*, the African krantz aloe, in downtown Yokohama in Japan, and pondering the underlying aesthetics and, of course, the pharmaceutical sensibilities of the person who placed it there.

In a way, this book was written on the go, while walking in foreign gardens or drinking coffee in quaint cafés in far-off cities. Gardeners who are fascinated by succulents tend to pay more attention to how these wonderfully versatile plants can be used in the process of transforming virtually any landscape, elevating them from the commonplace to the exceptional.

When carefully observing with the aim of creating a garden, one soon learns never to become too self-assured. Put simply, plants often do not want to be dictated to. However, part of the satisfaction of gardening with succulents is that they are easy to work with, and can swiftly transform derelict desolation into a desirable garden.

Essentially, all that is required is layers of personal imagination and some hard manual work

CACTI AND SUCCULENTS HANDBOOK

before finally settling back to celebrate the results. But before you get carried away with landscaping options, get to know your garden and be aware of its limits, taking cognizance of the size, shape, aspect, and slope of your property.

There is a strong trend toward viewing gardens and plants as significant investment pieces. Gone are the days when the average gardener was satisfied with acquiring some annuals to provide a few weeks of ephemeral color and beauty, then ripping them out and replacing them with the next season's crop.

The modern horticultural trend is aimed at beautifying a garden with plants that do not need to be watered and pampered every day. As environmentally friendly, water-wise gardening techniques become more widely established, sturdy, longer-lasting plants are coming into their own. Durable plants mean lower maintenance, which translates into less time spent caring for them, as well as less expenditure.

URBAN DESIGN TRENDS

Few other plants offer as many opportunities for creating solid, bold shapes and contrasting textures as cacti and succulents. For sophisticated, intense surface decoration, nothing delivers better than a dark-colored background created from crushed stone, gravel, or pebbles alternated with the bright green bodies and yellow spines of globular or columnar cacti.

A species such as *Echinocactus grusonii*, the Golden Barrel, comes into its own in an urban landscape as it provides the perfect slant on fashionable garden surface layering for a plush urban sanctuary.

Potted solutions

A collection of potted cacti is always eye-catching, and does not have to be perfect—it is more about the character of the grouping than the pedigree or origin of the plants.

All potted gardenscapes essentially have three elements to work with:

* The horizontal surface on which they are placed (for example, a patio or paved area);
* The vertical backdrop against which they will be viewed (such as a trellis, wall, or unobstructed, open vista);
* The three-dimensional shape of the containers and plants themselves.

All these elements must combine credibly to make a container collection visually appealing.

In the case of a group of potted cacti, less is usually more. In other words, it is wise not to clutter a background with intricate designs or too many diverse plants. Cacti are excellent architectural plants that require very little additional adornment to make a bold and attractive display statement.

A distinct benefit of container gardening in the

For a modern, minimalist twist on exterior wall decoration, single stems of *Cleistocactus samaipatanus* were established in clay pots attached to metal clamps.

Tried and tested, clay and terracotta pots work well for hardy cacti species, whether planted outdoors or indoors.

21st century is the vast range of pots that are readily available from garden centers and retailers.

With these, and the large number of cactus and succulent plants available from garden centers, it is easy to create virtually any atmosphere in your potted garden collection.

For example, to create a rustic feel, stick to the tried and tested clay pots. Although they are heavier than plastic ones, their porosity allows them to "breathe" more readily, and succulents and cacti generally grow and do very well in them.

Containers should all have clean, uncomplicated lines in order to show off the interesting shapes and textures of the various cacti and succulents, but the plants' versatility extends to the countless possibilities for growing them in containers of different materials and colors, from unglazed clay pots to bright, modern plastics.

However, when it comes to selecting a pot or any other container, the overriding consideration must be the porosity of the material from which it is made. If your garden is in a high-rainfall area, your outdoor pots must be made of very porous material, such as fired clay. This will allow the soil

mixture to dry out rapidly, limiting or preventing the loss of a prized specimen to rot.

In areas with low air humidity, highly porous pots would be detrimental to plant growth. Under such conditions, it is better to use plastic containers, as the high density of the material prevents evaporation of moisture through the pot.

It is always wise to determine the approximate eventual size of your chosen plant at maturity. Although many species can be easily bonsai'd into a stunted specimen with no ill effects to the plant, some, like large-growing agaves, will quickly outgrow a small container and look rather sickly. It is always better to start a plant in a pot that is large enough to allow it to grow for several years.

Water-wise gardening

Many parts of the world have an arid or semi-arid climate with daily and/or seasonal extremes such as very high and very low temperatures, and erratic and unpredictable rainfall. Predictably, many of the most popular horticultural subjects will not flourish in near-desert conditions. However, even in areas where rainfall is higher,

CACTI AND SUCCULENTS HANDBOOK

water is increasingly a precious commodity that requires wise and careful management.

Gardeners can play a significant role in water conservation by growing plants that need little water to look their best. Even in low-rainfall regions, it is possible to establish a cacti and succulent garden that is not only water-thrifty, but hosts a wide selection of different colors, textures, and forms.

Gardening for color

Cacti and companion succulents can be successfully used in a myriad ways to enhance specific gardening themes.

For a sparkling golden garden, try combining these succulent plants, all of which have variously yellow-margined or yellow-centered leaves: *Agave americana* var. *striata* and var. *marginata*, *Peperomia clusiifolia* "Jewellery," and the variegated forms of *Yucca guatemalensis* and *Portulacaria afra*.

For extra effect, match them with the following yellow-flowered plants: sculptural *Agave wercklei* (which only flowers after about eight years), shrubby *Aloe arborescens* (yellow form), climbing *Aloiampelos tenuior*, scrambling *Senecio tamoides* (canary creeper), or the miniature treelike *Senecio*

decaryii from Madagascar.

By contrast, using blue flowers and foliage in a garden introduces a degree of timeless antiquity. The leaves of numerous species of succulents are various shades of gray or blue (some quite intense), which makes for the possibility of creating a marvelous "lunar landscape." Plants with gray foliage tend be cooler than their green allies, as the light color reflects the rays of the sun, which in turn limits water loss, making these plants perfect for water-wise succulent gardening.

The following species are examples of plants with blueish leaves: *Agave americana* var. *americana* (massive rosettes), *Agave mitis* var. *albidior* (dense clusters of medium-sized rosettes), *Aloe glauca* (the small rosettes are borne on a short stem covered in the remains of dead leaves), *Echeveria lilacina* (small compact rosettes), and *Senecio crassulaefolius* (soft, pencil-shaped leaves borne in whorls on thin stems).

The last mentioned species, a succulent daisy, must rate as one of the most useful blue-leaved ground covers available in the horticultural trade.

A brief burst of golden-red aloe flowers offsets the cool greens of this array of succulents.

The main purpose of the *Cacti and Succulents Handbook* is to familiarize readers with a selection of some common and not-so-common, cacti and succulent species.

Special emphasis is placed on the Cactaceae, the flowering plant family in which all species of cactus are included. In the following chapters, a selection of easy-to-grow cactus species is discussed under the following headings.

Scientific name. As a general rule, a single scientific name is given per species, despite many species having multiple alternative names due to reclassifications over the years, as a result of an increase in our knowledge of relationships among species.

Only a few alternative or older scientific names are provided, and these are restricted to names that are still in common use, even though the species is nowadays differently classified.

Common name(s) where they exist. Although common names are not very accurate, they are often descriptive and interesting, with vivid images conjured up by names such as Silver Dollar, Bishop's Cap, Star Plant, Silver Torch, and Queen of the Night.

Not all species have common names, but all known plant species have scientific names.

Growing conditions. In the color bar below the name of each cactus species, symbol(s) indicate their relative hardiness in cultivation. More than one symbol implies that successful cultivation depends on the prevalent climate in your area. To be safe, it would be wise to first keep plants under the milder of the two conditions indicated. Refer to the symbol chart on page 37.

For the succulent plant families, the introductory notes to each family contain broad comments on cultivation.

Characteristics. Brief descriptions covering the stems, spines, and flowers, as well as other prominent characteristics, such as growth form, will assist in identifying the species.

Location and climate. This refers to the ideal microenvoronment where a species should be grown in order for it to thrive and flower.

Natural habitat. This information often gives additional clues on how and where to grow a particular species.

Number of species recognized in the genus. This gives an indication of the comparative size of the genus in which the species is included, and therefore how many close relatives it has.

The number of species recognized in a particular cactus genus has been taken from the excellent checklist of currently accepted names of Cactaceae produced by David Hunt as well as *The New Cactus Lexicon* that he coauthored.

Notes. Where relevant, additional notes are included on the species or its generic relatives (for example, its horticultural value or uses).

Although the bulk of the book is about cacti, it includes details of some easy-to-grow representatives of horticulturally useful, succulent "companion plant" families. The selected species will complement your cactus collection, enhance their beauty, and generally emphasize and show off their attributes through contrasting and/or complementary shapes, sizes, and colors. They are discussed alphabetically, according to families, genera, and species.

This book does not intend to be comprehensive. To achieve that, a multi-volume tome would be required, given that there are thousands of cacti and succulent species globally (particularly if one includes those species with succulent features that are not commonly cultivated). The intention here is rather to offer a selection of striking species included in some of the more popular cactus and succulent plant families.

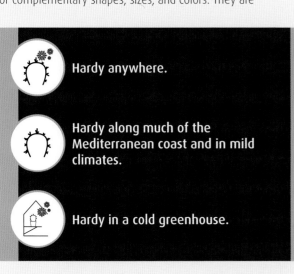

Hardy anywhere.

Hardy along much of the Mediterranean coast and in mild climates.

Hardy in a cold greenhouse.

Suitable for a greenhouse kept frost free.

Suitable for a greenhouse at a minimum of 50°F (10°C).

Cacti come in a wide variety of shapes and with varying types of spines.

COMMON SPECIES OF CACTI

The shapes and sizes of cacti fascinate horticulturally wise observers. Their massive ribbed trunks, fluted, globular plant bodies, thumb-sized stems, or scrambling growth forms conjure up images of what they will look like in a garden. Even before they produce their stunning blooms, they capture attention with their bold and often symmetrical outlines. Cacti are often highly prized specimen plants, but beware: initial interest can rapidly develop into an all-consuming passion and obsession!

The species in this section have been selected to illustrate the vast range of plant morphologies available, but there are over 1,800 species to choose from to start or expand your collection.

Number of species: 6

Common name: This alludes to the lifeless look of the plants, especially during times of severe moisture stress.

Description: Plant bodies are very small—between 1–3 in. (3–8 cm) in diameter—and hardly protrude above ground in their natural habitat.

Tubercles radiate almost horizontally from the stem base and are fairly long for such small plants, giving them the appearance of a small *Agave* species. The tubercles may carry a few small spines near their tips.

The flowers are a pleasant bright pinkish purple, even though the petals are edged with white. The flowers are very large for such small plants and, when young, almost entirely obscure the insignificant plant bodies. Plants flower in late summer to autumn.

Notes: The plant bodies of *Ariocarpus agavoides* are decidedly uncactus-like. At first sight they look like small plants of a rosette-forming species, and it is only on closer examination, especially when they flower, that it is apparent the plants belong to the cactus family.

This is not a species you will often encounter in your local nursery. In fact, Living Rock plants are not very easy to keep when they rely on their own roots for sustenance. However, when grafted onto an easy-to-grow relative, such as the shrubby cactus weed, *Quiabentia verticillata*, the plants grow exceedingly well and will flower while still very young.

Location: They prefer a sunny position and a well-drained soil mixture. However, if grafted onto another cactus, the plants will respond well to most cultivation conditions.

When kept on their own roots, these plants need to be watered sparingly. Take care to trim away any growth that the grafting stock may produce.

Natural habitat: Tamaulipas and San Luis Potosí in Mexico.

Two plants of *Ariocarpus agavoides* grafted onto a rootstock of *Quiabentia verticillata*, which is much easier in cultivation.

Number of species: 4

Common name: The name comes from the plant's resemblance to a bishop's cap (mitre), especially when viewed from above.

Description: The plant body starts out as angled-globular but, with age, it tends to become cylindrical-columnar, although the apices of the plant bodies are always distinctly depressed.

The stems are grayish green and sometimes have a purplish hue in full sun, but are almost entirely covered with minute whitish flecks. The plants remain unbranched. The fairly large areoles are tightly packed along the ribs, but do not bear any spines.

The flowers are bright yellow, tinged with red, and look a lot like those of mesembs (ice plants or midday flowers) or non-succulent daisies. They arise from the center of the "cap-like" body of the plant and open during the day.

Notes: With its densely white-flecked stems, this is a strikingly beautiful plant in cultivation. It is very easy to distinguish from other species of *Astrophytum* as a result of the body looking so much like a bishop's cap.

An attractive horticultural feature of the species is that the stems lack spines.

Location: For the species to look its best, it should be grown in a bright, sunny position. When it suffers from excessive water stress and high levels of solar radiation, it may turn a rather deep purple color.

Astrophytum myriostigma does not take kindly to temperatures below 32°F (0°C). Propagation is from seed.

Natural habitat: Central and northern Mexico, where is it widespread on the plateaus and high ground.

The spineless ribs of this old specimen of
Astrophytum myriostigma are spirally twisted.
The plant body has a pleasant purplish color.

Number of species: 1

Common name: The three common names for this archetypal cactus, which is shown in virtually every Western movie ever produced, are given above.

Description: Giant Cactus plants have thick, erect, multi-ribbed, solitary stems with a few vertical side branches mostly arising in the upper two-thirds.

The thick secondary branches in turn support sets of erect or variously curved smaller branches. In silhouette, this gives the plants a distinctive candelabra-like appearance, not unlike a cowboy ready to draw his guns!

In their natural habitat, Saguaro truly tower over other plants and can grow to gigantic dimensions, reaching a staggering height of over 65 ft. (20 m) and weighing up to nine tons. The ribs are armed with short, grayish brown needlelike spines.

The inner petals of the flowers are whitish, while the outer ones are greenish. The flowers, which open at night, appear in late spring to early summer.

Notes: The Saguaro plays an important role in the ecology of the deserts in which it occurs. Among other things, it provides food and shelter for many birds and animals.

Carnegiea gigantea is not common in cultivation, but no book on cacti would be complete without it.

The Saguaro National Monument near Tucson, Arizona, was established exclusively for this majestic cactus, whose flower is the state flower of Arizona. This genus contains only a single species, *Carnegiea gigantea.*

Location: Saguaros are incredibly slow-growing, taking 20 years or more to attain a height little more than half a yard. Only the most dedicated of collectors will attempt to grow this species. If you plant one when you are a youngster you may see it in flower—after you retire!

Furthermore, it makes a rather nondescript pot plant that requires quite some attention to ensure that it stays alive. Material is not easy to come by, but if you do locate plants to grow, keep them in containers, away from too much rainfall.

Although they can readily survive temperatures of 23°F (-5°C), they should not be exposed to prolonged periods of frost.

Natural habitat: Desert areas in Arizona and southern California (USA), and Sonora state in Mexico.

The creamy white flowers of *Carnegiea gigantea* appear in the late spring to early summer.

Varying ages of *Carnegiea gigantea* in the Sonoran Desert in Arizona in the southwestern USA.

Number of species: 3

Common name: No English common names have been recorded for the species. In Spanish it is known as *cardón blanco*. It is also sometimes known as *organo*.

Description: Plants are columnar, usually unbranched and can reach a height of about 32 ft. (10 m). The light green stems are almost entirely covered with dense clusters of spines.

The areoles carry dense groups of white, hair-like spines and a laterally situated pseudo-cephalium, especially near the tips of the stems.

The ribs are prominent and appear cross-furrowed, as a result of the regularly spaced areoles. The flowers are white to a light yellowish white color and flared open at their tips.

Notes: The imposing height that these plants can reach makes them quite spectacular in their natural habitat, where they form forests, and in cultivation.

Location: Plants grow fairly slowly and will be happy in a container for a long time. The soil mixture, in containers or in open beds, should always be well drained.

Natural habitat: Puebla, Mexico.

The areoles of *Cephalocereus columna-trajani* carry a dense covering of white hairs, especially near the tip of the stems.

COMMON SPECIES OF CACTI

43

Number of species: 25

Common name: This alludes to the nocturnal opening of the flowers.

Description: The plant body of this columnar cactus consists of numerous pole-like, pale blueish green stems. They are deeply ribbed and bear numerous woolly areoles from which bunches of sharp, needlelike spines arise.

The species flowers from late to midsummer. The large, pale white to creamish flowers are short-lived and open at night; a sure indication that they rely on bats for pollination.

Notes: This large, columnar cactus is well-known, even in areas remote from its natural habitat. The main reason for this is its ability to rapidly become established, often as an invasive alien, in areas that approximate the growing conditions in its country of origin.

In some parts of the world it is illegal to cultivate Cereus species as a result of its aggressive growth and spreading rates. In some respects, it is a pity that it grows so aggressively, as it is a striking accent plant.

The monstrose form of *Cereus hildmannianus* subsp. *uruguayanus* is particularly popular in collections. This is not surprising as the stems look uncannily like large lumps of molten wax strung together to form an oversized, columnar candle.

The numerous miniature forms of this species grow easily into attractive, softly spiny plants. The color of the spines of these variations could be yellow, white, or brown.

Location: The species should ideally be grown in full sun, but it also does well in semi-shaded positions. Before planting, investigate local legislation on alien plant invaders to make sure that it is not illegal to grow this species.

Country of origin: From southern Brazil, through Uruguay, to Argentina, South America.

The stems of this aberrant form of *Cereus hildmannianus* subsp. *uruguayanus* have the appearance of molten candle wax left to dry.

Cleistocactus samaipatanus

(also widely known as Bolivicereus samaipatanus *and* Borzicactus samaipatanus*)*

Number of species: About 40 species of *Cleistocactus* are currently recognized.

Common name: None recorded.

Description: Plants have rather thin, clump-forming, sprawling stems that remain erect for a short growth period only before they topple over.

The stems, which easily strike root where they touch the ground, are light green and multi-ribbed, with thorny areoles regularly arranged along the length of the stems.

The flowers are a bright crimson red color, with an elongated shape that is perfectly adapted for bird pollination. The tips of the petals are typically flared open and do not remain closely adpressed, as is often the case with the flowers of *Cleistocactus* species.

Plants tend to flower throughout the year, with a peak in summer.

Notes: Plants can be tied to a stake with a strip of soft fabric, such as a thin stretch of bicycle tire tubing.

This will prevent undue damage to the stems, but more than likely will only prevent stems from sprawling for a short time, as it interferes with their natural tendency to creep along the ground and up into surrounding vegetation.

Flowers that have not been pollinated quickly dry out on the plants and can be carefully removed to yield year-round, tidy-looking plants.

Location: The preferred method of propagating *Cleistocactus samaipatanus* is undoubtedly through stem cuttings. In fact this is one of a number of cactus species that the average grower will probably never have to attempt from seed.

After allowing a few days for the cut surface to dry out, the cuttings can be planted directly in the ground at the preferred site.

Once established, plants will thrive in full sun and in dappled shade. If it gets overgrown by other plants, the occasional stem will periodically appear through the surrounding foliage before it once more topples over to the ground. In this way plants of this species continue their zigzag march across a bed, a habit that has its own horticultural charisma!

Country of origin: Santa Cruz, Bolivia.

The crimson red flowers of *Cleistocactus samaipatanus* are perfectly shaped for bird pollination. Unlike the flowers of the majority of *Cleistocactus* species, the flower tips are flared open.

Number of species: About 40 species of *Cleistocactus* are currently recognized.

Common name: "Silver Torch" is an allusion to the densely spined, silvery tipped stems of the species.

Description: Plants form shrubby clumps consisting of a number of fairly slender, erect stems of up to 6½ ft. (2 m) tall. In this, and related species, the stems may topple over in the course of time, or arch onto the ground, where they will become rooted and continue their growth.

The stems have multiple ribs that are adorned with numerous areoles from which dense bunches of dainty, needlelike spines arise.

The upwardly pointed but apically down-curved flowers are borne almost horizontally and are carried on the sides of the upper third of the stems. The flowers are quite robust, deep red, and have long, straight tubes with the tips of the petals slightly spreading. They are borne in spring and summer, but some clones of this species flower throughout the year.

Notes: This beautiful species will flower profusely once mature (when it is ± 3 ft. /1 m tall). Even as seedlings, the species warrants cultivation because of the striking silvery color imparted to the stems as a result of the densely packed spines.

The flowers with their long funnels are indicative that the species relies on visits from birds rather than insects for successful pollination.

Location: The species thrives in bright, full sunshine. It does well as a potplant or in the open garden. In fact, most species in the genus are very easy to grow.

Place of origin: Santa Cruz, Bolivia, and northern Argentina.

The stems of *Cleistocactus strausii*, which remain erect for a long time before toppling over under their own weight, are densely covered with thin, white spines.

Number of species: About 40 species of *Cleistocactus* are currently recognized.

Common name: No common names are recorded for the species.

Description: The plant body consists of multibranched, columnar, ribbed, light green stems that can reach a height of about 3 ft. (1 m).

The spines are densely and rather neatly distributed along the margins of the ribs and very sharp, arising from series of small, white areoles. The spines vary slightly in color from brick red to golden brown.

The flowers are tube-shaped, somewhat resembling lit cigarettes, except that the tips are yellow and the tubes are red!

Notes: This is a most desirable species to grow as a feature plant in open beds, although it will also thrive in containers. The allure of the species lies in its neatly arranged reddish brown spines that appear to be of two lengths.

Location: The species is propagated very easily from stem cuttings. It grows well in cultivation and will give years of pleasure in a pot before it is necessary to replant it.

These plants will tolerate subzero temperatures for short periods of time. They require little aftercare, apart from the almost universal cactus-need for bright sunlight.

Natural habitat: La Paz in Bolivia.

The young growth near the stem tips of *Cleistocactus varispinus* carries slightly longer, golden brown spines. The spines lower down the stems are also needlelike, but shorter.

Number of species: 9 species are currently recognized in the genus *Consolea*.

Common name: No common names are recorded for the species.

Description: Plants usually consist of a single, columnar stem that branches densely from the top to form a large, loose canopy. Single plants can reach a height of well over 26 ft. (8 m). The stems become cylindrical with age and carry dense clusters of sharp spines.

The elongated, somewhat egg-shaped stem segments are flattened and a shiny bright green. These stem segments are virtually spineless.

Flower color varies from yellow to orange, turning deep red with age. Flowers are produced in summer.

Notes: This species grows as a most imposing tree. It is most distinctive as a result of the densely spiny stems, dark green stem segments and orange-red flowers. It is exceptionally popular as a curiosity plant and is sure to be an interesting talking point in any cactus collection.

Location: *Consolea picardae* thrives in full sun. It can be grown in the open ground or in any size container. It does very well as a potted plant and will happily grow in a small pot for many years before it needs to be repotted.

However, it is unlikely to produce flowers if its root and stem development are restricted by a container.

Natural habitat: Hispaniola.

Consolea picardae grows as a typical cactus tree, forming an open canopy consisting of stem segments strung together like a string of large, egg-shaped beads.

Cylindropuntia fulgida var. *fulgida* (also known as Opuntia fulgida)
Chain-Fruit Cholla

Number of species: About 30 species are currently recognized in *Cylindropuntia*.

Common name: Chain-Fruit Cholla, referring to the fruit of this species that are linked together like a chain of beads.

Description: Treelike plants with numerous branches that form a medium-sized, spreading canopy. The dull green stems are multi-ribbed and very spiny. The yellowish spines are carried in clusters on areoles situated on raised protuberances, giving the stems a somewhat warty appearance.

The flowers, which open in the late afternoon, are a purplish color.

Notes: Although plants are somewhat variable, it is generally easy to identify them as a result of the dull green stem color, yellowish, radiating spine clusters, and raised stem protuberances. However, the best way of identifying them is by means of the chains of greenish yellow fruit that appear after flowering.

If plants are grown in a greenhouse, care should be taken that it is kept away from pedestrian traffic as the stem segments become dislodged very easily if one bumps into the spines. And the spines are sharp enough to cause pain and discomfort!

Location: Cultivation is primarily through stem cuttings. To bring out the best in this species, it has to be given free root-run in an open bed.

It is exceptionally hardy and prefers full sun and can tolerate severe cold and drought. Care should be taken that the species does not spread into the natural environment away from its habitat, as it tends to become weedy.

Place of origin: Sonoran Desert of Arizona (USA) and northwest Mexico and Baja California, Mexico.

The fruits of *Cylindropuntia fulgida* var. *fulgida* are attached to one another end-to-end, giving rise to the common name, Chain-Fruit Cholla.

Cylindropuntia imbricata (also widely known as Opuntia imbricata)
Candelabra Cholla

Number of species: About 30 species are currently recognized in *Cylindropuntia*.

Common name: Candelabra Cholla, alluding to both the branched and rebranched growth form of the species. The species is also known as devil's rope cactus, which refers to the knotty shape of the branches that look like woven rope.

Description: This medium-sized to large, shrubby species can reach a height of up to 6½ ft. (2 m). The stem segments are cylindrical and grayish green, with prominent stem tubercles. The tubercles carry yellowish areoles that in turn produce yellowish to reddish brown spines.

The bright purple flowers are produced in spring and early summer.

Notes: In contrast to the other species of *Cylindropuntia* discussed, the stem segments of *Cylindropuntia imbricata* are not obscured by its spines, as these are generally shorter, but not less menacing, than in the other species. Many species of *Cylindropuntia*, including *C. imbricata*, have become invasive weeds in places very remote from their natural habitats. Unwanted material should therefore not be discarded where it could become established.

Location: The species prefers bright, sunny positions, making it perfect for cultivation in large gardens or in a greenhouse with sufficient bench space. It is one of the most tolerant cactus species in cultivation and will withstand much neglect and abuse.

Propagation is by means of stem cuttings, which root quite easily.

Natural habitat: The southern USA and Mexico.

The flowers of *Cylindropuntia imbricata* are a striking bright purple color.

Cylindropuntia tunicata
Sheathed Cholla

Number of species: About 30 species are currently recognized in *Cylindropuntia*.

Common name: Sheathed Cholla, alluding to the persistent spine sheaths.

Description: Plants grow as small to medium-sized, multibranched shrubs. The stems are a dull, light green, but, especially during times of drought, are almost entirely obscured by the spines, that are carried in dense clusters on prominent tubercles that resemble the rudder of a small boat.

The spines are yellowish white, needlelike, and very pungent. Each spine is enveloped in a sheath.

The flowers are a light yellow-green.

Notes: Many species of cactus are beautiful even when not in flower. With its densely clustered, light-colored spines, this species certainly is one of them.

Location: For successful cultivation this species requires little more than full sun and an occasional watering.

It grows exceedingly easily from stem cuttings that root rapidly where they are planted or simply dropped, a clear indication that it can become a weed.

Country of origin: Northern parts of Mexico.

The clusters of yellowish white spines of *Cylindropuntia tunicata* contribute to the beauty of the species, even when it is not in flower.

Number of species: 11 species are currently upheld in *Disocactus*.

Common name: Rat's Tail Cactus, alluding to the long, dangling stems that appear hairy and taillike as a result of the dense covering of short, bristly spines.

Description: The pale green, elongated drooping stems of this species are up to 1 in. (2 cm) in diameter, but in cultivation they tend to be somewhat thinner.

In time the stems could reach a length of almost 6½ ft. (2 m). The finely ribbed stems are adorned with soft, rather nonpungent spines that will cause little more than some discomfort when the plants are handled.

Clusters of stems will rapidly dangle over the edge of a container. In most clones the spines are a beautiful golden color giving the plants a glowing yellow sheen. The flowers are fairly large for the comparatively thin stems and are bright pink to red.

They appear in spring and summer and open by day.

Notes: This is one of a number of cacti that is perfect for cultivation in hanging baskets.

Although stem cuttings can take a while to root (sometimes up to one year), plants grow very quickly once roots have formed. The stems are sturdy enough to withstand the occasional unsuspecting passerby bumping into them, and the spines do not become dislodged from the plant as easily as is the case with many other species of cactus.

In its natural habitat these plants grow as epiphytes on trees or in rock crevices.

The species flowers readily in the spring and summer months. When in flower the upper parts of the stems are virtually covered in a mass of bright reddish or pinkish blooms.

Location: Plants do best in baskets that are hung in semi-shady positions that receive bright light. They provide protection against frost damage if it is grown in below-zero temperatures.

Natural habitat: Oaxaca and Hidalgo, Mexico.

The flowers of *Disocactus flagelliformis* are a striking reddish to purple color. With its long, dangling stems, the species is perfectly suited to cultivation in a hanging basket.

Echinocactus grusonii
Golden-Barrel Cactus

Number of species: 6 species are included in *Echinocactus*.

Common name: Golden-Barrel Cactus, alluding to the size and shape of the plant body that looks like a small wine vat.

Another common name is Mother-in-Law's Armchair (or seat or cushion), which refers to the sharp thorns covering the plant body and, rather unkindly, to the apparent tendency of some husbands to "torture" their mothers-in-law!

Description: Plants develop into large barrels with a height of about 3 ft. (1 m) and a spread of over 20 in. (50 cm).

The stems will in time offset from the base to form large clumps. The stems have multiple ribs that are densely adorned with beautiful, very sharp, golden yellow spines but, true to the variation so prevalent in cacti, there are also forms of the species that have almost pure white or even very short spines or that may lack them altogether.

The tops of the barrels, where the flowers are produced, are cushioned with a soft, yellow furry substance.

The decorative flowers appear in spring and summer and are a vibrant yellow that almost hurts the eyes in bright sunshine. Even the dry, brown flowers that remain on the plants are decorative.

Notes: This species is extremely common in cultivation, and millions of plants are produced annually for the horticultural trade. It must also rate as one of the most photographed species of cactus in the world as a well-grown, mature specimen is invariably a showstopper. It can easily grow to about two to three times the size of a soccer ball, but if growth is limited in a container, almost like a bonsai tree, it will give years of pleasure as a windowsill plant.

Location: Plants prefer bright, sunny positions and can tolerate fairly low temperatures. The species is extremely easy to grow.

Natural habitat: Querétaro, Mexico.

In this bed in the Huntington Botanical Gardens, several magnificent clusters of *Echinocactus grusonii* perfectly frame the blue-leaved *Agave parryi*.

Number of species: 6 species are included in *Echinocactus*.

Common name: Giant-Barrel Cactus, alluding to the exceptional size that this species can attain. It has the shape and size of a wine vat.

Description: Plants develop into very large, ribbed barrels with a height of about 6½ ft. (2 m) and a spread of nearly 3 ft. (1 m).

The number of ribs on a stem varies greatly. The ribs are covered with very sharp spines that can vary in color from yellow through light reddish to nearly black in older specimens.

As with *Echinocactus grusonii* (the common golden barrel cactus), the tops of the barrels, where the flowers are produced, are cushioned with a soft, yellow furry substance. The bright yellow flowers are quite large and appear in spring and summer.

Notes: This species is not as common in cultivation as its relative, *Echinocactus grusonii*. However, it grows fairly quickly in cultivation and will, in time, take on fairly large, barrel-like dimensions.

Location: Plants do best in full sun. The species does not pose any problems in cultivation, provided it is given good drainage and a friable soil mixture.

Natural habitat: Coahuilla and Puebla in central and northern Mexico.

The spines of *Echinocactus platyacantha*, the largest of all the barrel cacti, are crossbanded, shorter than those of *Echinocactus grusonii*, and usually dark brown.

Close-up of the golden-yellow flowers of *Echinocactus platyacantha*.

Echinocereus engelmannii
Dagger-Spine Hedgehog

Number of species: Almost 70 species are recognized in *Echinocereus*.

Common names: Numerous common names have been recorded for the species, including Dagger-Spine Hedgehog, in reference to the shape and sharpness of the spines.

Description: Plants usually form a multitude of stems, often up to 50, to give rise to medium-sized to massive clumps. The dull green stems are distinctly ribbed and carry very sharp, creamy white spines, which are borne horizontally or point downward.

Flower color varies from purple red through bright purple.

Notes: What the flowers of some forms lack in terms of size, they more than make up for in color. In fact, the color of the flowers, usually a bright, shiny purple, makes this a very desirable species to grow. The stems shrink when the plants are subjected to water stress, making the spines appear even more densely arranged.

Location: Plants thrive in full sun and will grow quite quickly if grown in open beds. Propagation is by means of stem cuttings or from seed.

Natural habitat: The species is exceedingly common in southwestern USA and northwestern Mexico.

The flowers of *Echinocereus engelmannii* are a deep purple color, contrasting sharply with the creamy white spines. Some forms of the species, such as this one, have smallish flowers, but the color remains a striking purple.

Number of species: Almost 70 species are recognized in *Echinocereus*.

Common name: No common names are recorded for the species.

Description: Plants grow as small clumps that consist of numerous stems that can reach a height of about 20 in. (50 cm), but in cultivation they tend to be somewhat shorter.

The ribs on the stems can be adorned with distinct tubercles or they can be fairly smooth. The stems of the subspecies *morricalii* are more or less spineless.

The bright purple flowers, which open during the day, are borne in midsummer.

Notes: When in flower, this is one of the most spectacular of the medium-sized species of cactus in cultivation, and justifiably so: the plants are easy in cultivation, spines are virtually absent, flowers are readily produced, and they are a near-fluorescent purple.

Location: While still small, this is another one of the cactus species perfect for windowsill cultivation.

The plants will thrive in almost any potting soil and flower in profusion if given a bright, sunny spot and sufficient water. The species does equally well in a rock garden, where it will grow much faster.

Natural habitat: Nuevo León in Mexico.

As far as flower color is concerned, the intense, glistening purple of the flowers of *Echinocereus viereckii* subsp. *moricalii* is difficult to beat, even among cacti.

Number of species: About 80 species are currently recognized in *Echinopsis*.

Common name: Peanut Cactus, a reference to the size and shape of the stems that resemble the closed pods of a peanut.

(*Echinopsis chamaecereus* is widely known as *Chameacereus silvestrii* and *Lobivia silvestrii*; but it should not be confused with *Echinopsis silvestrii*, a different species with white flowers.)

Description: The densely clustering stems of this miniature cactus are generally up to 8 in. (20 cm) long, but in cultivation they tend to vary from 1½–2 in. (3–5 cm) in length. They are pale green and covered in small clusters of fine spines. Although quite prickly, the spines do not readily become detached from the stems, making the plants easy to handle.

The flowers are a magnificent bright shade of orange-red and up to 2 in. (5 cm) in diameter. These fairly large flowers are formed in spring and early summer and open during the day.

Notes: The Peanut Cactus is one of the first species that any collector of cacti ever acquires. Over the years, numerous slightly more robust hybrids have been produced, with this species as one of the parents. They all have superior flowers and stems in terms of both size and color.

Location: Plants do best in full sun, either as container plants or in open beds. The species is exceptionally easy to cultivate and will thrive in virtually any type of soil. It will also tolerate subzero temperatures for surprisingly long periods of time.

The stems become detached from a plant quite easily and will root where they fall.

Natural habitat: Tucumán, Argentina.

The flowers of the miniature *Echinopsis chamaecereus* are a pleasant crimson red and are produced in profusion when the plant is cultivated. This species is exceedingly common in cultivation.

Number of species: About 80 species are included in *Echinopsis*.

Common name: No common names are recorded for the species.

Description: Plants branch from the base and grow as medium-sized to large clumps of erect or creeping stems. The stems are distinctly cylindrical and can reach a height of nearly 3 ft. (1 m). The stems are ribbed and usually a light green color. The edges of the ribs are adorned with golden brown spines that project straight outward from the areoles.

The flowers are quite large, up to 3 in. (7 cm) across, and tend to be funnel-shaped. Flower color varies from red through orange to yellow.

Notes: This must rate as one of the most rewarding species of cactus to grow. The short, straight, radiating spines adorning the edges of the ribs are very decorative and form a striking contrast with the light green color of the stems. The flowers are intensely colored and always appear brilliantly shiny, regardless of whether they are red, orange, or yellow.

Location: This is one of the easiest of cacti to grow, and hardly any effort is required to have a really striking cactus in cultivation.

The species is easily propagated from stem cuttings that root without any difficulty. It looks its best when grown in full sunlight.

Natural habitat: The northern parts of Argentina.

With age, the stems of *Echinopsis huascha* tend to lean against rocks or surrounding plants. The flowers of this easy-to-grow species vary from bright yellow to orange and even red.

Number of species: There are about 12 species in *Epiphyllum*.

Common names: Rick-Rack Orchid Cactus or Fishbone Cactus; both names refer to the interesting structure and shape of the stems of this species. Another common name, Moon Cactus, refers to the fact that the whitish flowers open at night.

Description: The drooping leaflike stems that can reach a length of several feet are characteristically deeply indented along their margins, giving them a zigzag appearance. The stems lack thorns and are flattened, except low down where they are somewhat thickened. The areoles on the stem margins occasionally bear a few bristles.

On the inside, the flowers are bright white, but externally they are a yellow or golden color. The long-tubed flowers are borne in the summer months and open at night. Strikingly beautiful pink-flowered forms are also more rarely encountered.

Notes: Although the stems of many of the leaflike species of cactus are not particularly striking in their appearance, *Epiphyllum anguliger* is an exception. The deep invaginations of the stems give the plants a strange, almost otherworldly look. The species is often shy to flower in cultivation.

Location: These plants should be kept away from direct sunshine otherwise they will certainly suffer from sun-scorch. Indeed, the stems turn a beautiful vibrant green color if kept in well-shaded positions, adding to the fascination of the plant.

Epiphyllum anguliger requires a friable, compost-rich soil mixture. It benefits from occasional feeding with a liquid fertilizer.

Natural habitat: Central and southern Mexico.

After fertilization, the flowers of *Epiphyllum anguliger* are replaced by small, bright green fruit. The plant does very well in a hanging basket.

A form of *Epiphyllum anguliger* with purplish-infused flowers.

Number of species: 34 species are included in *Eriosyce*.

Common names: No common names are recorded for this species.

Description: The plants are small and globose in shape and a delightful light green color. The plant body consists of small tubercles that each carry a set of beautifully recurved, light yellow to golden yellow spines.

The flowers are a bright purple color. The plants tend to flower at any time of the year, and the flowers open during the day.

Notes: Plants look like small, fluffy balls of thorns, especially when water is in short supply. This is a delightful species, as the flowering period is not restricted to any one season and one can therefore count on having flowers at any time of the year, even during winter.

Location: Given that the species comes from a fairly arid area, it somewhat surprisingly requires no special treatment in cultivation.

As usual, care should be taken not to overwater the plants, especially in the summer months.

Natural habitat: The Chilean coast.

Top. When young, the plant bodies of *Eriocyse subgibbosa* var. *litoralis* are almost entirely obscured by the dense layer of beautiful golden yellow spines.

Right. The flowers of *Eriosyce subgibbosa* var. *litoralis* are a bright purple color that contrasts sharply with the golden yellow spines.

Ferocactus cylindraceus subsp. *cylindraceus*
(also known as Ferocactus acanthodes)

Desert Barrel Cactus

Number of species: 28 species of *Ferocactus* are currently recognized.

Common name: Desert Barrel Cactus refers to its arid habitat, and the shape of the plant body at maturity.

Description: Plants are mostly solitary and branch only very rarely. The plant bodies are rather elongated and barrel-shaped at maturity, but will remain globular or spherical if their growth is curtailed in a container.

The stems are distinctly ribbed and the edges of the ribs carry ferocious spines, some of which are recurved. The spines are round or flattened and vary in color from white to red, yellow, or brown.

The flowers are uniformly yellow, or sometimes tinged with red. They are produced in spring and summer and open by day.

Notes: The genus *Ferocactus* contains some of the most beautiful and desirable cacti to grow, despite the fact that they are very slow-growing, take many years to mature, and the plants tend to remain solitary.

With its ferocious spines, *Ferocactus cylindraceous* var. *cylindraceus* develops into a particularly striking specimen. The dense bunches of brilliantly colored hooked spines are especially attractive. Over time, they almost entirely cover the light green stems, forming a striking contrast.

Location: The species is easy to cultivate in a container or open beds. It does best in a sunny position and does not need protection against the fierce afternoon sun.

This species will not tolerate very wet conditions, so the soil in a container should be allowed to dry out completely between waterings.

In its natural habitat it can be huge (up to 10 ft./3 m tall), but in cultivation it tends to remain considerably smaller.

Natural habitat: Widespread in parts of southern California, southwestern Arizona (USA) and Sonora state in Mexico.

The stems of *Ferocactus cylindraceus* var. *cylindraceus* are barrel-shaped and covered with sharp, reddish, recurved spines.

Number of species: *Ferocactus* is a genus of about 28 species.

Common name: Fire Barrel Cactus references the dense covering of red spines, and the shape of the plant body at maturity.

Description: Plants are solitary and can reach a height of well over 10 ft. (3 m). The plant bodies are elongated and barrel-shaped when mature, but will remain globular or spherical at first, especially if their growth is curtailed in a container.

The stems are distinctly ribbed and the edges of the ribs carry ferocious spines, some of which are dagger-like recurved and viciously hooked. The spines are round or flattened and mostly distinctly red. Some spines are somewhat papery, hairlike, and whitish in color. The flowers are a deep orangey red. They are produced in spring and summer and open during the day.

Notes: With its dense covering of ferocious spines, *Ferocactus gracilis* subsp. *gracilis* is truly eye-catching.

Location: The species is easy to cultivate in a container or open beds. It does best in a position that receives maximum sun. Care should be taken that plants are not overwatered. Let the soil dry out between irrigations. In its natural habitat it can be huge, but in cultivation it tends to remain considerably smaller.

Natural habitat: Baja California, Mexico.

Some of the spines on the rib margins of *Ferocactus gracilis* subsp. *gracilis* are dagger-shaped and viciously hooked downward.

Ferocactus histrix

Mexican Barrel Cactus

Number of species: *Ferocactus* is a genus of about 28 species.

Common name: The common name Mexican Barrel Cactus references the wide occurrence of the species in the central parts of that country, as well as the shape of the plant body at maturity.

Description: Plants are solitary and reach a height of about 3 ft. (1 m), but usually remain smaller. The plant bodies are cylindrical to globular with a slight depression on top.

The stems are distinctly ribbed and the edges of the ribs carry an almost continuous row of areoles that are armed with short to medium-sized spines, some of which are down-curved and slightly hooked. The spines are round or flattened and vary from yellowish to reddish-brown. The flowers are yellow. They are produced in spring and summer and open during the day.

Notes: This is one of the most widespread barrel-shaped cacti in Mexico. It does not grow quite as tall as some of the other species included in *Ferocactus*, but nonetheless has a barrel-shaped plant body at maturity. In some of the Mexican states where the species occurs, cooked mature floral buds are eaten, for example when prepared with scrambled or fried eggs.

Location: The species is easy to cultivate in a container or open beds. Plants will thrive in full sun, but will also tolerate dappled shade. As always, bear in mind that the growing medium should not be allowed to become water-logged. At maturity, plants are more manageable in size than some of the other barrel cacti.

Natural habitat: *Ferocactus hystrix* is widely distributed across central Mexico, including in Hidalgo, Jalisco, San Luis Potosí, and Zacatecas.

Flower buds of *Ferocactus* species, such as *F. histrix* and *F. pilosus* (shown here), are pickled and bottled in Matehuala, San Luis Potosí, Mexico.

The flowers of *Ferocactus hystrix* are a bright yellow color and arranged in a ring near the tip of the barrel.

Number of species: 28 species of *Ferocactus* are currently recognized.

Common name: Crow's Claw, a reference to the shape, size, and arrangement of the broad, flat spines.

Description: The light green plant body is flat-globular to spherical and can grow to about two to three times the size of a soccer ball (±12 in./30 cm high with a spread of ±20 in./50 cm).

The stems usually have a slight depression at the top, are ribbed, and the ribs are adorned with broad, flat, hooked spines that will in time curve backward toward the stem.

The spines are banded and could be various shades of red, yellow, or cream and are very decorative. But beware, they are also very sharp and pungent!

Flower color varies from purple to off-white or yellowish. Flowers appear in summer and open during the day.

Notes: This barrel-shaped cactus is very desirable to cultivate, particularly as a result of its beautiful spines. It is not the only species of barrel cactus with brightly colored and banded, recurved spines, but it is probably the most widely cultivated species with spines that have these traits.

It is very slow-growing and can be kept in a large container for many years before it will be necessary to transplant it.

Location: For best results the species should be planted in a bright, sunny position in a rock garden. If it is kept in a container, this should be placed in a position that receives adequate sunlight.

Although *Ferocactus latispinus* will take several years to produce its first flowers, the spines are very decorative, making the wait for flowers much easier.

Country of origin: Widespread in central Mexico.

The flowers of *Ferocactus latispinus* var. *latispinus* come in various shades of purple and red, with dark centers.

Ferocactus pilosus
Mexican Lime Cactus

Number of species: 28 species of *Ferocactus* are currently recognized.

Common name: Mexican Lime Cactus, alluding to the occurence of the species on limestone cliffs. (It is not restricted to this substrate, however.)

Description: Plants start their lives as small, ball-shaped plant bodies, but in time form large, rather narrow, barrel-shaped cactus plants. Plants remain solitary or will, in time, give rise to large clumps through basal sprouts.

   The barrels can reach a height of nearly 10 ft. (3 m), are a light green color and deeply ribbed. The rib margins carry densely arranged areoles that give rise to clusters of strikingly beautiful dull red to crimson spines. Flower color varies from yellow-red to bright red.

Notes: This is one of the most striking of all cacti. The young spines at the tips of the stems are a magnificent red, almost putting the small yellow to red flowers to shame as far as color is concerned. As is the case with many species of barrel cacti, the flowers are produced in a ring around the tips of the stems. The fruits are edible and have an acidic taste.

Location: Plants prefer full sun and a well-drained soil mixture. Plants grow rather slowly in cultivation, but with some patience will form striking barrels, even in a greenhouse.

Country of origin: The high deserts of northern central parts of Mexico.

The red of the spines at the tips of *Ferocactus pilosus* stems are even brighter than the color of the flowers.

The ribs on the stems of *Ferocactus pilosus* are covered with longitudinal series of sharp spines.

Number of species: 42 species of *Gymnocalycium* are currently recognized.

Common name: Chin Cactus.

Description: These plants are usually globular, but may in time become somewhat globose-columnar. The stems are a striking grayish coppery green, but the color is not quite as intense as *Gymnocalycium mihanovichii* and *Gymocalycium stenopleurum.*

The plant bodies are distinctly ribbed, but again the valleys between the ribs are not as deep as in the Plaid Cactus. The ribs are somewhat invaginated (folded in on themselves) and are adorned with seemingly harmless clusters of short, recurved, off-white spines.

Flowers are white or a very delicate shade of pale pink and are produced during the summer.

Notes: The decorative spines resemble small, white-legged spiders. The species is very common in cultivation and flowers freely.

Location: This easy-to-grow species makes a perfect subject for potting. It stays fairly small in cultivation and is best kept in a container.

Natural habitat: Córdoba, Argentina.

Gymnocalycium quehlianum is yet another very common species in cultivation. Its ribs are not as sharply angled and the areoles carry fewer spines than those of *Gymnocalycium mihanovichii*. The flower buds are typically club-shaped.

Number of species: 42 species of *Gymnocalycium* are currently recognized.

Common name: Plaid Cactus, referring to the somewhat checkered coloring and appearance of the stem-patterning.

Description: This globular species has a beautiful, crossbanded, almost copper-colored stem, especially in good light positions. Plants are usually solitary, but small plantlets may slowly form near the base of the stem.

The ribs are adorned with short, stubby spines that usually curve back toward the plant body.

The developing flowers are club-shaped and have the same strange copper color as the stems. The outer segments of the flower buds overlap symmetrically, giving them a very tidy appearance. Flower color varies from a soft hue of pink to light yellowish or green. The species flowers in summer and the flowers open during the day.

Notes: Since the species does not attain the same stem dimensions as some of the other globular to spherical cacti described here, it is perfectly suited for container cultivation, as it flowers easily and profusely, even when still fairly small.

The related *Gymnocalycium mihanovichii,* which is commonly known as plaid cactus, is the mother material from which the so-called Ruby Ball cacti have been developed. The stems of these cultivars are any color but green and must always be grafted onto a green mother stock to ensure that they will survive. *Gymnocalycium stenopleurum* has also been called *G. mihanovichii* var. *friedrichii* or simply *G. friedrichii,* but the correct name at species rank is *G. stenopleurum.*

Location: The species does best in semi-shady positions where bright, filtered sunlight will bring out its best colors. It is very easy in cultivation and will thrive in virtually any type of soil. They flower easily, even when still fairly young.

Natural habitat: Bolivia and Paraguay.

Gymnocalycium stenopleurum is one of the most common species in cultivation. It is likely that many cacti collections were started with this species only.

Number of species: *Harrisia* currently includes about 10 species.

Common name: Moon Cactus, a name used for many night-flowering species of cactus, having large, white blooms that open at night.

Description: The climbing, ropelike plant bodies are distinctly ribbed and can grow to about 6½ ft. (2 m) in length. The stems are unable to support their own weight and necessarily make use of surrounding plants or structures to support themselves.

The edges of the stems are variously adorned with small, white woolly areoles that are armed with widely but regularly spaced bunches of straight, yellowish gray spines.

In mid- to late summer a number of dainty pale white flowers are borne on the margins of the plant body. The red fruits are quite conspicuous and the size of a tennis ball.

Notes: Plants tend to scramble through vegetation, where the unsuspecting passerby could easily bump into them. The allure of the species lies in its large white flowers and the decorative red fruits.

The small, black seeds tend to germinate where they are dropped by birds, and the species can soon spread into areas where it is unwanted.

Location: This must rate as one of the easiest species of cactus to grow away from its natural habitat. It is not at all fussy as far as growth medium, watering regime, and exposure to sunlight is concerned.

It makes for an interesting potted plant that will look its best if grown in a quiet corner of a patio next to a support structure, away from regular pedestrian traffic. It will also thrive in open beds, especially if grown in strong, dappled sunlight under a deciduous tree. Propagation is from seed or stem cuttings.

Country of origin: Argentina.

Above. The large, white flowers of
Harrisia martinii open at night.

Right. *Harrisia martinii* has thick,
ropelike stems that are adorned with
sharp spines.

Hatiora salicornioides
Beer Bottle Cactus

Number of species: 6 species are recognized in *Hatiora*.

Common name: Beer Bottle Cactus, alluding to the stem segments that resemble small, inverted beer bottles.

Description: The thin, drooping stems of this epiphytic cactus are distinctly jointed and bright green, blotched with purple.

The stem segments really look like miniature beer bottles stacked one on top of another. The stems start out erect, but soon start to droop under the burden of their own weight. They are completely devoid of spines, soft and easy to work with.

The flowers are very small, but a beautiful bright yellow and are produced in profusion in spring and early summer.

Notes: The segmented nature of the stems of this species reminds one of the plant bodies of some seaweeds or species of the unrelated genus *Salicornia* (family Chenopodiaceae).

Location: This species is easy to cultivate if given a friable mixture containing course organic material, such as tree bark chips, sufficient water, and occasional liquid plant fertilizer. It struggles in full sunlight and requires a shady position. It can tolerate dry conditions if grown in the shade. Segments of the stems that become dislodged from the mother plant will rapidly set root and eventually vigorously overgrow it.

Natural habitat: Around Rio de Janeiro, Brazil.

Above. Close-up of the yellow flowers of *Hatiora salicornioides*.

Right. It is easy to see why *Hatiora salicornioides* is called the beer bottle plant: the shape of the small stem segments closely resembles that of miniature liquor bottles.

Number of species: 11 species are recognized in *Hylocereus*.

Common name: Scrambling Cactus, referring to the growth habit of this species.

Description: The stems of this species are a bright, glossy green and divided into distinct joints. The stems are angled, giving them a winged appearance. The plants branch freely and have aerial roots along the stem margins, making them well adapted for climbing onto supporting structures. They can easily grow to heights of 50–65 ft. (15–20 m) with adequate support. A few small, scattered thorns develop along the stem margins.

The flowers are very large, with white inner segments and yellowish outer segments, and open at night during midsummer.

Notes: This species is a very vigorous grower and has been known to smother large trees and collapse flimsy structures, so care should be taken as to where it is grown.

As a result of its strong growth, it is often used in frost-free areas as rootstock for cactus species that are difficult to grow on their own roots.

The large red fruits of *Hylocereus undatus*, known as dragon fruit, are delicious and the species is often cultivated specifically for this purpose.

Location: Plants should be planted at the bases of structures or trees into which they are intended to climb.

Bright sunny or dappled shady positions are preferred, and protection must be provided against frost. The species is not suitable for containers. The species has been known to escape from cultivation, especially in subtropical and tropical regions.

Natural habitat: The species has been widely introduced into cultivation and today it is difficult to establish where it came from originally.

Plants of *Hylocereus undatus* will in time form large masses of tangled stems that will twine onto surrounding plants.

Isolatocereus dumortieri (also widely known as Stenocereus dumortieri)

Candelabra Cactus

Number of species: This is the only species included in *Isolatocereus*.

Common name: Candelabra Cactus, alluding to the shape of the plant.

Description: These magnificent plants can attain a height of about 50 ft. (15 m). Large, thick branches are carried in a vertical disposition on a short trunk. The branches are distinctly ribbed and carry prominent areoles on their margins. Each areole carries a small cluster of spines.

The greenish white flowers are fairly small for such a large plant. They are tube-shaped and open at night.

Notes: This is a truly striking plant when seen for the first time. Its massive branches reach skyward from a short trunk that looks suspiciously incapable of supporting the candelabra-shaped crown.

Location: Given the size that these plants can attain, it is clearly suitable only for large gardens. Grown from seed, it will be happy in a container for a few years, but it requires ample root space in open beds to allow it to reach its full magnificent maturity.

Natural habitat: The species is widespread in several Mexican states, including Puebla, Oaxaca, and Hidalgo.

Old specimens of *Isolatocereus dumortieri*, such as the one depicted here, have numerous, large, robust branches that are carried vertically.

Number of species: Only a single species is recognized in *Leuchtenbergia*.

Common name: Agave Cactus, in reference to the resemblance it bears to *Agave*, the century plant.

Description: *Leuchtenbergia principis* has a very distinctive appearance for a cactus: it consists of a number of long, angular, slender tubercles that radiate out from the central stem of the plant.

The tubercles are gray-green and can reach an incredible 5 in. (12 cm) in length. At first glance the tubercles create the impression that plants consist of whorls of leaves. The leaflike tubercles will be shed in time, exposing a short stem with "leaf scars." The tips of the tubercles are adorned with stiff but fragile papery thorns.

Large pale to deep yellow or pinkish flowers are borne in spring and summer.

As this species has large, succulent roots, it is important to allow sufficient room for the roots to develop if the plants are grown in containers.

Notes: This species is one of the so-called "novelty cacti." It looks so very uncactus-like, especially when not in flower, that it is inevitably a plant to talk about when you show people around your greenhouse.

Location: The species is very hardy, and will tolerate a lot of abuse in cultivation. It prefers a sunny position where it can receive plenty of strong light. It tends to flower better if given sufficient water during the flowering season. Enough water will also prevent the tubercles from dying back at their tips. Although this is a natural phenomenon, it leaves the plant looking rather unsightly.

Natural habitat: The species is widespread in central and northern Mexico.

The bright yellow flowers of *Leuchtenbergia principis* are quite large, have a frilly appearance, and when the plants are young, will obscure most of the plant body.

The stem tubercles of *Leuchtenbergia principis* are elongated and carry the areoles at their tips. This species typically has a very uncactus-like appearance, rather resembling a species of *Agave*, the century plant.

Mammillaria compressa subsp. *compressa*
Mother of Hundreds

Number of species: At least 160 species are currently included in *Mammillaria*.

Common name: Mother of Hundreds, a very apt reference to the profusion with which the plants form offsets.

Description: Plants will in time form medium-sized to massive clusters of spherical to somewhat cylindrical stems with a diameter of up to 4 in. (10 cm). The dark green stems consist of numerous sturdy, nipple-like protuberances that carry very sharp spines that can be straight or curved like fish hooks.

The flowers are most commonly a bright purple color and are followed by bright pink or red, elongated fruits.

Notes: Species of the genus *Mammillaria* are perfectly suited for cultivation in small containers. They are generally very decorative, even when not in flower, as a result of their beautiful spines.

The flowers of *Mammillaria compressa* subsp. *compressa* are small but very decorative. In addition, the brightly colored fruit adds to its attractiveness in cultivation.

The spines are very sharp and will puncture the unsuspecting passerby, especially if the plants are grown near the edge of a plant table.

Location: This is one of the most popular species for growing on a windowsill. It will thrive in most soil types and is very easy in cultivation.

In summer it will flower in profusion if given sufficient sunlight.

Natural habitat: San Luis Potosi and surrounding states in Mexico.

Mammillaria compressa subsp. *compressa*, a widely cultivated species, produces a profusion of small red, very decorative flowers in near-perfect rings around the plant body.

COMMON SPECIES OF CACTI

Number of species: At least 160 species are currently included in *Mammillaria.*

Common name: Golden Star Cactus, alluding to the starlike appearance of the densely thorny stems when viewed from above.

Description: Plants form dense masses of short to medium-long tuberculed stems that are almost entirely covered with short spines. In fact, the color of the pale greenish stems is almost entirely obscured by the dense covering of spines that vary from pale creamish white to dark reddish brown. This is especially true if the plants suffer from drought stress that results in stem contraction.

The spines are soft and often slightly recurved toward the stems.

The flowers are light creamish yellow and appear in early summer.

Notes: If *Echinopsis chamaecereus*, the Peanut Cactus, is often the first species that a collector acquires, then *Mammillaria elongata* and the similar looking but white-spined *Mammillaria gracilis* are likely the second and third species to arrive in a collection.

Mammillaria elongata is exceedingly common in cultivation and a truly worthwhile initial addition to the collection of a budding cactologist.

As a result of the extreme variation in thorn color, it is quite possible to build up a small collection consisting almost entirely of variants of this species.

Location: One of the main reasons for the popularity of *Mammillaria elongata* in cultivation is the ease with which it grows and flowers.

Furthermore, the fact that one seldom sees the stems, as a result of their dense covering of spines, also makes it a worthwhile addition to any collection.

The plant is an extremely good grower that will thrive in pots or as specimens dangling over rocks and boulders. Bright sunlight brings out the best colors, but it will also survive in containers as windowsill plants.

Natural habitat: Hidalgo, Guanajuato, and Querétaro in Mexico.

Top. The small, yellowish flowers of *Mammillaria elongata* subsp. *elongata* are often somewhat hidden among the spines carried on the small tubercles.

Above. Although *Mammillaria elongata* subsp. *elongata* is best known among collectors as a miniature species grown as a windowsill plant, the stems can ultimately reach a length of about 12 in. (30 cm).

Raisin Cactus

Number of species: 4 species are currently included in *Myrtillocactus*.

Common name: Raisin Cactus, alluding to the edible, raisin-like dried fruit of the species.

Description: This treelike species with columnar stems can reach a height of up to 16 ft. (5 m). Plants are multibranched with the thick, grayish green branches gracefully curved upward from the stems and side-branches from which they arise. The stems are somewhat sparingly armed with small to medium-sized stout spines.

The flowers are greenish white and rather small and insignificant. Flowers are often produced in small clusters and are followed by small purple berries. The flowers are borne in summer and open during the day.

Notes: A mature *Myrtillocactus* plant will make a striking feature in a container or in a garden bed. It is also an interesting talking point, because the small, purplish fruits are edible and very tasty, although the tiny fruits, called garambullo, look out of place on such large plants.

Location: Plants should be grown in full sun. The stems tend to be thinner and a rather artificial-looking grayish blue color if they do not receive sufficient sunlight.

The species is easy to grow from seed or stem cuttings. Seedlings and immature specimens will thrive in small containers for many years before they need to be repotted.

Natural habitat: Central Mexico.

Myrtillocactus geometrizans flowers are small and light yellow in color (below), while the plants can reach substantial dimensions, growing as large as multibranched trees (right).

Number of species: 9 species are currently recognized in *Neobuxbaumia*.

Common name: Cone Cactus, a name of unknown derivation.

Description: Plants are solitary and columnar, forming a single, very stout stem up to 20 in. (50 cm) in diameter and 32 ft. (10 m) tall. The stem is light green and only very rarely produces side-branches, often where the stem was damaged.

The stems are distinctly ribbed and are armed with fairly short, needlelike spines. However, in the upper part of the stem where the flowers are produced, the spines tend to be up to 3 in. (7 cm) long.

The flowers are dark red and open at night in the summer months.

Notes: This is a massive species when mature. Magnificent specimens are anchored to the white cliffs of the Jardin Exotique de Monaco (see page 104), where the mild Mediterranean climate has brought out the best in plants that were established there almost 100 years ago. Today they form a magnificent backdrop for the multitude of other species of cactus grown in this magnificent botanical garden.

Location: This is a fairly easy species to cultivate, especially from seed, but it will take many years to reach maturity.

It will initially grow well in a container, but should ultimately be given its rightful place in a garden.

Natural habitat: The species is widespread in south-central Mexico.

This magnificent specimen of *Neobuxbaumia polylopha* towers over the companion plants with which it is grown.

Number of species: About 75 *Opuntia* species are currently recognized.

Common name: Prickly Pear, alluding to the edible fruit that is covered by very fine, bristlelike spines (glochids). The species is also called Mission Cactus, referring to its cultivation as a food crop in early mission stations in the western USA.

Description: The plants are treelike at maturity and form a short stem that branches higher up to form a dense crown of closely packed stem segments or pads.

The pads are always flattened and ferociously spined. The spines are sharp and needlelike, and are sure to cause harm to any unsuspecting passerby who bumps into them.

The beautiful yellow to orange flowers form on the edges of the pads and are borne in summer. In late summer these develop into large, juicy fruits with a multitude of small seeds embedded in a tasty pulp.

Notes: The species grows very easily and can rapidly outstay its welcome in an adopted country—so much so that it is considered one of the world's worst succulent plant pests. Take care not to allow it to spread. It can easily escape from domestic gardens and become an invasive pest plant in countries far from its natural habitat.

A spineless form has been selected and is today widely grown. The pads, or stem segments, of this cultivar are often used as a fodder plant.

Opuntia ficus-indica is cultivated more for its fruit than as a horticultural plant, even though a well-grown, mature specimen has a strikingly odd growth form. The fruit is edible, and is considered by some people to be a real delicacy, especially if it is cooked before eating.

Opuntia ficus-indica is important as a host plant for rearing cochineal insects. The female insects produce a natural dye of the same name, which is used in the food, drink, and cosmetic industries.

Location: In warmer climates, these plants are extremely hardy and will thrive in most situations, although they prefer full sun. They can tolerate a tremendous amount of horticultural neglect, and will keep on growing, flowering, and producing fruit.

Country of origin: Most probably central Mexico.

The economically important *Opuntia ficus-indica* yields delicious edible fruit, but it is also a noxious weed in some parts of the world.

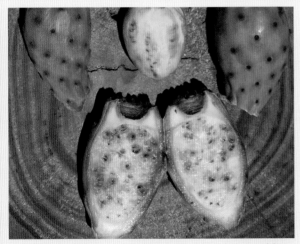

Prickly Pears, also know as Cactus Pears, harvested from *Opuntia ficus-indica* are regarded as a delicacy in many parts of the world.

This spineless form of *Opuntia ficus-indica* carries bright yellow flowers.

COMMON SPECIES OF CACTI

Number of species: About 75 species are currently recognized in *Opuntia*.

Common name: Eastern Prickly Pear, in reference to the species' natural distribution range in the eastern parts of the USA.

Description: Plants grow as medium-sized shrubs of about 12 in. (30 cm) tall, with numerous flattened pads, or stem segments, that appear to crawl along the ground. The stem segments are elliptical in outline and carry a number of scattered areoles that are adorned with small clusters of yellowish brown glochids. A few spines are produced on the upper sides of the pads.

The flowers are bright yellow, while the fruits are light green, tinged with a deep purplish pink.

Notes: Unlike most *Opuntia* species, the pads of this species often rather curiously lie flat on the ground.

Location: This species will survive in virtually any temperate conditions, being extremely cold hardy and even able to withstand being covered by a thin blanket of snow. It will tolerate most winters without protection, provided it has good drainage.

Country of origin: The eastern parts of the USA.

Opuntia humifusa can tolerate surprisingly cold and wet conditions for a species of cactus.

The flattened stem segments of *Opuntia humifusa* tend to sprawl along the ground. The fruits are a decorative purplish color.

Opuntia microdasys
Bunny Ears Cactus

Number of species: About 75 species are currently recognized in *Opuntia*.

Common name: Bunny Ears Cactus, alluding to the small, woolly pads that are covered in deceptively soft-looking glochids.

Description: Plants remain small and shrub-like for many years, after which small, treelike specimens are formed.

The pale green, flattened pads (stem segments) are comparatively small and lack the rather long, prominent spines that most species of cactus display.

However, the areoles carry thousands of small, barbed glochids that are arranged in dense bundles over the entire surface of the stem segments. The pale yellow flowers only form on mature plants.

Notes: The species is slow-growing, taking many years to reach the size of a small tree. The pads remain fairly small and are covered by small bunches of yellow (most common), brown, or pure white glochids. This striking color variation, encountered in the glochids of the species, makes it a desirable plant to cultivate and it is almost always available commercially.

These plants do not flower readily, and should be mature in order to produce their small yellow flowers.

Location: This cactus is exceptionally easy to cultivate and does well in almost any type of soil. But be sure to keep the plants away from areas of high traffic as the glochids become dislodged quite easily and will cause extreme discomfort to the skin.

Take care that it does not spread into natural environment where, in time, it will become a pest plant.

Natural habitat: Chihuahuan Desert of Mexico.

Opuntia microdasys flowers are a bright yellowish orange color.

The form of *Opuntia microdasys* with white glochids is arguably the most desirable to grow of the horticultural varieties available. The fruits turn a light purple color as they mature.

Number of species: About 75 species are currently recognized in *Opuntia*.

Common name: This alludes to the color of the stem segments.

Description: Plants grow as medium-sized to large mounds up to 6½ ft. (2 m) wide and high. The plant bodies consist of numerous flattened pads that are round in outline. The stem segments are a delightful purple color.

Only very few brown spines are produced per areole, but these small, cushion-like structures carry prominent, golden brown glochids.

The large yellow flowers with reddish bases are borne in the summer months.

Notes: The most striking feature of *Opuntia santa-rita* is undoubtedly the wonderful purple color of the stem segments. This color becomes more intense under conditions of environmental stress, such as a lack of water.

Location: This is arguably one of the most desirable of the *Opuntia* species, as a result of the color of its pads. Not only is it a beautiful plant, but it is also a curiosity in a garden.

It requires well-drained soil and will flourish in an open bed or a container. It will grow well even if somewhat pot-bound and will flower regularly, even after years in a container.

Natural habitat: Arizona, Texas, and New Mexico in the USA; Sonora state in Mexico.

The stem segments of *Opuntia santa-rita* are a bright purple color, while the flowers are a strongly contrasting bright yellow.

Oreocereus celsianus

Old Man of the Andes

Number of species: Six species are currently recognized in *Oreocereus*.

Common name: Alluding to the thick, silky white hair that envelops the stems, giving the plants a "senior citizen" appearance.

Description: Since the stems of this species branch from the base, old plants form erect, candelabra-like specimens.

The erect, columnar stems can reach a height of up to 6 ½ ft. (2 m) in their natural habitat:, but in container cultivation they rarely exceed 3 ft. (1 m). The stems have numerous closely packed ribs that are adorned with sharp, thin, needlelike spines. Most of the stem length is enveloped in thickly-set woolly hair.

The flowers, which arise laterally from near the stem tips, are medium-sized and light purple to pink.

Notes: This is another cactus species that has a thick bush of white hair wrapped around its stems. It may look inviting to stroke the hair, but beware: it harbors very sharp thorns.

Oreocereus celsianus is rather slow-growing and will do well in a small container for many years.

Do not hold your breath for blooms, as only mature specimens tend to flower regularly.

It can be separated from the other similar-looking species included in this book, *Cephalocereus columnatrajani* (see page 43), by virtue of the fact that the hair tends to be longer and not set as close to the stem. *Cleistocactus strausii* also looks like this species, but it never has the mane of woolly hair.

Location: It grows well in bright sunlight, but for the hottest part of the day should be provided with some dappled shade protection to prevent sun-scorch damage. It is perfect for container cultivation on a shaded patio or verandah.

While it can tolerate slight frost, the plants should be kept fairly dry in wet winters to prevent them from rotting. In cold climates, it is best to cultivate them in an unheated greenhouse.

Natural habitat: Bolivia, Peru, and Argentina.

The columnar stems of *Oreocereus celsianus* are covered in symmetrically arranged spines that are almost entirely hidden by dense tufts of white hair.

Number of species: Six species are included in *Oreocereus*.

Common name: Alluding to the bunches of grayish white, woolly hairs carried terminally on the stems.

Description: Plants proliferate from the base and, over time, will form large clumps. The stems can reach a height of up to 3 ft. (1 m) and have fairly shallow ribs.

The rib margins carry prominent grayish white, circular areoles from which a number of sharp, needlelike, reddish brown spines arise.

Especially toward the upper parts of the stems, the areoles also carry fairly dense tufts of grayish white, silky hairs and frizzy gray wool. However, in contrast to numerous other species, the hairs do not quite envelop the stems; they rather tend to stand out from the areoles, imitating a hippy on a bad hair day!

The somewhat tubular flowers appear in the summer months from a cephalium and are a beautiful crimson red. The tubes of the flowers are very narrow, scaly, and hairy.

Notes: This species is not cultivated primarily for its flowers. Although the flowers are indeed showy, the true attraction lies in the woolly stems. Once it reaches flowering maturity, the stems tend to become thicker toward their apices. Propagation is from cuttings.

Location: *Oreocereus doelzianus*, and indeed also the other species included in the genus, thrives in bright sunlight. However, it will tolerate some shade without becoming etiolated.

Cultivated plants have been known to tolerate winter temperatures of down to 23°F (-5°C), provided they are kept dry; in an unheated greenhouse (hothouse) if necessary.

Natural habitat: Ayacucho in central Peru.

The flowers of *Oreocereus doelzianus* are a bright purple color.

The spines and hairlike coverings on the stems of *Oreocereus doelzianus* are fairly short and do not obscure the stems.

Mexican Fence Post Cactus

Number of species: 13 species are recognized in *Pachycereus*.

Common name: Alluding to the practice of planting this cactus along fence lines.

Description: Majestic single- or multistemmed specimens, forming striking bright, light green treelike columns. The stems are ribbed, with the edges of the ribs adorned with white areoles that run into one another, forming a continuous band.

Most commonly the spines are fairly short, but very pungent. The flowers are reddish and funnel-shaped.

Notes: Although the stems are planted as living fences and fence posts in their native Mexico, the average gardener is likely to appreciate them more for their architectural shape.

Like the majority of cactus species, the spines are very pungent, but as they are rather short, the plants can be handled easily.

Location: This must rate as one of the fastest-growing species of columnar cactus. They prefer full sun, which will bring out the beautiful green color of the stems. Plants grow easily from stem cuttings, which is certainly the preferred method of propagation.

Natural habitat: The species is widely distributed in central Mexico.

Right. Plants of *Pachycereus marginatus* produce only a small number of ribs. The margins of these are adorned with short, stout spines.

Far right. Some older specimens of *Pachycereus marginatus* often have tall, vertical branches that tower skyward.

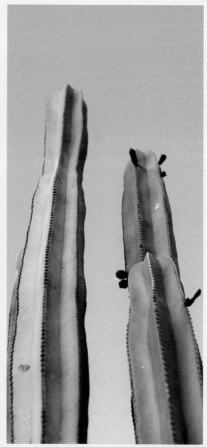

Number of species: 13 species are recognized in *Pachycereus*.

Common name: Elephant Cactus, Mexican Giant Cardon.

Description: In their natural habitat, these plants are treelike and their erect columnar stems can reach a height of more than 32 ft. (10 m).

The pale blueish-green stems are distinctly ribbed and have neat rows of almost-white spines arranged along the edges. As is the case with some treelike species, the stems of this species also become more or less spineless with maturity.

The flowers are fairly large and white, and open during the day and night. The fruit is edible but very spiny.

Notes: Although this is one of the largest-growing cacti encountered in cultivation, it is most often available as fairly small seedlings or immature plants. This means that the plants will remain manageable in containers, or even open beds, for many years.

Plants can indeed be grown in fairly small containers where they will thrive and, effectively, become "bonsai'd" (reduced in size), apparently with no ill effect to them. Once planted out into open beds they grow into large, multibranched clumps.

It has been proposed that the *Pachycereus pringlei* should be transferred to the genus *Lophocereus*, as *Lophocereus marginatus*, but the species is here retained in the genus *Pachycereus*.

Location: This species is exceptionally hardy in warm climates and will thrive in most positions in a garden. Provided the plants are not given too much water in winter, they will tolerate fairly low temperatures.

Plants are mainly grown from seed, as cuttings seem to be too thick and unwieldy to work with.

Natural habitat: Mexico, particularly the states of Sonora, Nayarit and Baja California.

With age, *Pachycereus pringlei* carries very tall branches and its ribs are rather smooth.

Pachycereus schottii (also known as Lophocereus magnifica)

Whisker Cactus, Totem Pole Cactus

Number of species: 13 species are recognized in *Pachycereus*.

Common name: Senita cereus or Whisker Cactus, alluding to the long spines borne on the edges of the ribs. The name, Totem Pole Cactus, is applied especially to the monstrose form of the species, alluding to the somewhat segmented and highly ornamental appearance of the stems. (Monstrose means that some of the species characteristics become abnormal, such as the stems being devoid of spines.)

Description: Plants branch from near ground level to form large treelike clumps, or shrubs consisting of numerous columnar branches.

Stems can be erect, or may topple over and root along the edges where they touch the ground. The stems are a beautiful pale yellowish-green color and are deeply ribbed. The edges of the ribs are armed with numerous blackish thorns up to 1½ in. (3 cm) long.

Flowers are produced laterally from a terminal pseudo-cephalium that may carry bunches of long, broom-hair-like spines. The inner segments of the flowers are pinkish red, while the external segments are green.

Flowering takes place at night during the summer months.

Notes: Two monstrose forms of this species are very popular in cultivation. The first has thick, smooth, and nearly thornless stems, while the stems of the other one are often twisted and thinner with less pronounced ornamented segments. Both develop into strikingly beautiful accent plants.

Location: The species will grow equally well in bright, direct sunlight and in semi-shaded positions. Especially the monstrose form of the species is very hardy in cultivation, as well as pest resistant.

Country of origin: Baja California and Sonora in Mexico; southern Arizona in the USA.

The regular form of *Pachycereus schottii* has a profusion of sharp spines on the margins of the ribs.

The monstrose form of *Pachycereus schottii* often has fantastically twisted stems that resemble candle wax art.

Number of species: About 60 species are included in *Parodia*.

Common name: No common name is recorded for the species.

Description: Plants usually form solitary, globular, or slightly cylindrical light green stems. However, with age, the plants will slowly form offsets to give rise to multiheaded clumps.

The stems are distinctly ribbed and carry numerous neatly spaced areoles on the rib edges. The areoles look like small woolly cushions, from which clusters of sharp, needlelike, yellow or brown spines arise.

Flower color varies somewhat, from yellow with deeper orange sections, to reddish or purplish.

Notes: In some forms the woolly areoles are prominent, giving the plants a very decorative appearance. The strongly contrasting orange or reddish flowers arising from the white, woolly areoles make this a desirable species to grow.

Location: This sun-loving species should be given ample natural light conditions to look its best. It grows well in a container or in open beds. However, plants will also grow well in partial shade. Plants are frost sensitive and should be kept dry during the winter resting period. As with most cacti, the growing medium should be well drained.

Country of origin: The species occurs naturally in the Rio Grande do Sul, Brazil.

The areoles of some forms of *Parodia horstii* are densely adorned with white wool. The flowers are fairly small, but carried in profusion.

Number of species: About 60 species are included in *Parodia*.

Common name: No common names are recorded for the species.

Description: The plants grow as clusters of short to medium-length, cylindrical columns. The stems are densely ribbed and carry neat rows of closely and regularly spaced areoles along the rib margins. The spines are light yellow to golden brown.

The flowers are golden yellow and borne in profusion at the tips of the stems. The flower petals have slight invaginations (folds or indents) at their tips giving them an interesting, somewhat frilly appearance.

Notes: This must rate as one of the most popular cacti in greenhouse collections. When young, the plants look uncannily like those of the related *Parodia magnifica*, but *Parodia leninghausii* grows taller, and its stems are more cylindrical in outline, with more ribs.

Location: The plant does well in containers but, to allow it to reach bigger dimensions, it should be given free root-run in an open bed. It grows very easily from seed or cuttings.

It can tolerate temperatures of just below freezing.

Natural habitat: Rio Grande do Sul, Brazil

The stem tips of *Parodia leninghausii* carry dense clusters of brown spines that contrast pleasantly with the white wool of the areoles and golden-yellow spines on the older parts of the stems.

Parodia magnifica (also widely known as Notocactus magnifica)

Yellow Ball Cactus

Number of species: About 60 species are included in *Parodia*.

Common name: Yellow Ball Cactus, alluding to the color of the flowers and spines, as well as its somewhat ball-shaped plant bodies.

Description: Plants form small to large clusters of almost spherical light green to blueish green stems which are distinctly sharp-ribbed, with stiff, but feathery-looking spines along the ribs.

The spines arise from a series of confluent (merging) areoles, which gives the edges of the ribs a white appearance, that later turns yellow. The spines vary in color from bright yellow to white.

The flowers are usually bright yellow, but a form with lemon yellow flowers is also known. Flowering takes place in midsummer, during the day.

Notes: The stems of this species have a nasty habit of splitting if the plant is overwatered. The resulting rather unsightly wounds will eventually heal, but are difficult to hide and can disfigure the plants permanently.

However, it is one of the more rewarding cactus species to grow, as it is easy in cultivation, readily producing numerous, large yellow flowers at the center of the body of the plant.

Location: This is a fairly hardy cactus species, and will thrive in extreme conditions. It can be kept dry for a long time without any apparent damage to the plant. It also tolerates very low temperatures, if dry.

It thrives in containers and also in open beds.

Natural habitat: Rio Grande do Sul, Brazil.

The ribs on the stems of *Parodia magnifica* carry dense rows of fairly soft, yellow spines. The large flowers are bright yellow.

Number of species: 17 species are currently recognized in *Pereskia*.

Common name: Barbados or West Indian Gooseberry, a reference to the small, yellow berries that appear after the flowers. However, the species is not in the least related to true gooseberries (family Grossulariaceae). It occurs naturally in many Caribbean and northern and southern American countries, not only Barbados.

Two less frequently encountered common names are Rose Cactus, referring to the resemblance it bears to rose bushes in flower, and Lemon Vine, referring to its fragrant flowers.

Description: Plants are typically huge bushlike shrubs or woody climbers with long, flexible branches. The semi-permanent leaves are large, flat and semi-succulent and look very much like those of a typical shrub or tree.

Plants branch freely and will rapidly spread into and onto any surrounding vegetation or supporting structure.

The stems and branches are fairly soft and succulent and armed with pairs of short, hooked, very pungent (sharp-pointed) spines. Older stems are woody and bear bunches of long, straight spines.

The fragrant flowers are borne from autumn to midwinter and vary from white through creamish to yellow, or even pink. The flowers are eventually replaced by small, scaly, green berries that turn yellow or orange when ripe.

Notes: The uninitiated can be forgiven for mistaking this species, especially when it is young, for a bougainvillea or rose bush, or any other shrub for that matter! It does not in the least look like a cactus, especially with its large leaves and open, rose-like flowers.

The flowers are strongly lemon-scented and quite attractive.

Location: The species thrives in tropical and subtropical environs. It grows so fast in the open that it soon smothers surrounding vegetation, becoming a pest plant.

For this reason, it should not be cultivated in tropical or subtropical areas where it can become an invasive alien. In cold climates, however, it should be protected against subzero temperatures.

The species is often used as a rootstock on which difficult-to-grow or threatened species of cactus are grafted.

Natural habitat: The species occurs in Florida (USA), the West Indies, Brazil, and Paraguay. In some areas it is difficult to ascertain whether it is indigenous or has escaped from local gardens.

The leaves of the horticultural selection of *Pereskia aculeata* known as 'Godseffiana' have purple and creamy white blotches.

Number of species: 17 species are currently recognized in *Pereskia*.

Common name: The species is often referred to by its scientific epithet, *Sacharosa*, which means "rich in sugar."

Description: Plants have a treelike or robust, shrubby growth form. The stems are fairly thin and carry numerous areoles along their lengths. These are adorned with vicious, very sharp spines.

The leaves are more or less egg-shaped in outline and tend to be folded laterally along their midribs.

The rose-like flowers are various shades of pink and purple. They are replaced by fleshy, yellowish fruit.

Notes: The young spines are a striking bright red color. But, make no mistake, once they have become hardened, they are extremely pungent.

As is the case for most species of *Pereskia*, care should be taken that it does not spread into areas where it can become weedy, typically those where the prevailing environmental conditions approximate those encountered in its natural habitat.

Location: Plants prefer full sun or dappled shade. They grow very easily from stem cuttings, which is the preferred method of cultivation.

Natural habitat: The species is indigenous to higher-lying parts of Brazil, Bolivia, Paraguay, and Argentina.

Top. *Pereskia sacharosa* flowers are rose-like in appearance and come in various shades of pink or purple.
Above. The young spines carried on the areoles of *Pereskia sacharosa* are a striking reddish color.

Whip Cactus

Number of species: Two species are included in *Quiabentia*.

Common name: The branches of this tree-like shrub are fairly thin and whip-like. If one bumps into the spines, it stings like being hit with a whip.

Description: Plants grow as large, treelike shrubs. The stems are fairly thin and a deep green color, irregularly dotted with small, white areoles. The leaves are bright green and distinctly succulent. They remain on the plant for a long time before being shed. Leaf shape varies from oval to daggerlike, and they are always blunt-tipped.

The small pale reddish pink flowers are produced throughout the summer months, but surprisingly not in great profusion if grown away from its natural habitat.

Notes: The stems are fairly brittle and break easily if attempts are made to twine them through a trellis.

The plant can easily be trimmed with a pair of pruners (secateurs) if it becomes unwieldy and overgrown. Take care, however, that the spines, which are easily dislodged from the plant, do not puncture the gardener! *Quiabentia verticillata* is sometimes included in the genus *Pereskia*.

Location: Plants grow exceedingly easily from seed and stem cuttings; in fact, so easily that care should be taken not to allow it to spread as it has a tendency to become weedy in temperate and subtropical regions.

As it prefers high temperatures, it is not often grown in colder climates.

Natural habitat: The species is widespread in the arid regions of Bolivia, Paraguay, and Argentina.

The leaves of the rather uncactus-like *Quiabentia verticillata* are very succulent.

Rhipsalis baccifera subsp. *mauritiana*
Rope Cactus

Number of species: 36 species are included in *Rhipsalis*.

Common name: Rope Cactus, a reference to the thin, string-like stems of the species.

Description: The straw-like stems are thin and wiry, and arise from the central growing point of the plant. In time, a thick cluster of stems forms, which branch profusely after they have elongated for ±4–6 in. (10–15 cm).

The rather pale green stems are almost smooth, with only a few hairs, unlike the stems of some related species that are densely adorned with fluffy white hairs to protect them from excessive sunlight.

The flowers are fairly small, whitish and insignificant. The fruits are a similar almost translucent white color. The fruits remain attached to the stems for many months, making them quite decorative.

Notes: The flowers of most species of *Rhipsalis* are fairly insignificant, but what they lack in terms of flower color they more than make up for through their rapid growth and interesting, ropelike stems.

Species of *Rhipsalis* grow as epiphytes in trees, often in high-rainfall forests. The growth medium in which they are planted should therefore be well drained, but rich in nutrients.

Location: Most species of *Rhipsalis* will benefit from protection against excessive sunlight. They prefer shady positions that approximate the conditions under which they grow in nature. There are few cactus species are better adapted to being grown in hanging baskets.

Natural habitat: This species has the widest geographical distribution range of all known cacti. It occurs in the Americas (North, Central, and South), Africa, Madagascar, and Sri Lanka.

The stems of *Rhipsalis baccifera* subsp. *mauritiana*, here dangling from a tree fork, are thin and wiry.

Rhipsalis baccifera subsp. *mauritiana* is the only known cactus regarded as indigenous to the African continent.

Rhipsalis mesembryanthemoides
Mesemb Cactus, Ice-Plant Cactus

Number of species: 36 species are included in *Rhipsalis*.

Common name: Mesemb Cactus or Ice-Plant Cactus, referring to the resemblance that the species bears to some representatives of the predominantly southern African succulent plant family Mesembryanthemaceae, the Ice-plants, or Fig-marigolds.

The species forms thin, wiry, bright green stems that are usually densely covered in bunches of fairly short side-segments.

The stems are erect at first, but will in time start to droop. The areoles on the stems do not bear any spines, only a few soft white bristles.

The flowers, which are borne on the short stem segments, are fairly small and a rather insignificant white to off-white color. The fruits are also white.

Notes: Although people may scoff at cultivating this cactus species with its ropelike stems, it is fast-growing and very rewarding.

Location: This is a perfect hanging basket plant whose stems will dangle over the edge of a suspended basket and provide year-round greenery on a verandah. It requires a semi-shaded position, some air humidity, and regular feeding as it often grows in the forks of trees where there are plenty of decaying leaves and other sources of natural fertilizer.

Natural habitat: Rio de Janeiro, Brazil.

The ropelike plant bodies of *Rhipsalis mesembryanthemoides* resemble those of some species of the southern African "midday flower" family, the Mesembryanthemaceae.

Rhipsalis mesembryanthemoides flowers are small and yellowish white, but what this species lacks in terms of flower color, it makes up for in the total number of flowers it produces.

Number of species: 36 species are included in *Rhipsalis*.

Common name: No common names are recorded for the species.

Description: Plants grow as drooping or half-erect shrublets. The older stems tend to be either cylindrical or three-angled, while the young stems emerging from the stem tips are distinctly flattened. If grown in dappled shade, the stems are light green, while those exposed to direct sunlight take on a pinkish hue. The margins of the segments are slightly wavy. The small areoles carry tiny clusters of harmless glochids.

The flowers are very small and light yellow in color.

Notes: At first sight, *Rhipsalis oblonga* may be confused with a specimen of *Schlumbergera*, the Christmas or Easter Cactus. However, once it has produced its small, insignificant flowers, there is no doubt that it belongs to *Rhipsalis*.

Location: Like most *Rhipsalis* species, this one is perfectly adapted for cultivation in a hanging basket. Once a stem segment inserted directly into the soil has become rooted, the emerging stem segments will soon dangle over the side of a container.

The plants are not cold tolerant and must be protected from subzero temperatures. Hanging baskets should be positioned to avoid direct sunlight.

Natural habitat: The species is indigenous to Brazil.

The light yellow to creamy white flowers of *Rhipsalis oblonga* are lacy and quite delicate.

The young, drooping stem segments of *Rhipsalis oblonga* are distinctly flattened, while the older ones tend to be cylindrical. The flowers are small and an insignificant yellowish-green.

Schlumbergera truncata
Christmas Cactus

Number of species: Six species are included in *Schlumbergera*.

Common name: Christmas Cactus, alluding to the fact that the species flowers prolifically from November to January in the northern hemisphere.

In the southern hemisphere, these species are often called Easter Cacti, as they tend to have a second, somewhat briefer, flowering period during the early autumn.

Description: The plant bodies are much-branched and consist of jointed series of small, shiny green, leaflike pads that are flattened and, to some extent, resemble miniaturized forms of the pads of some of the more common opuntioid cacti. The margins of the stem segments are fairly deeply indented, producing prominent but harmless outgrowths.

The flowers are very large for the fairly small plant bodies and a dazzling bright pink, red, orange, or white. The upper and lateral segments of the flowers are strongly reflexed, adding to their beauty and fluffy appearance.

Notes: The species is often used in the production of hybrids, which produce flowers in even greater numbers than the pure species. The sensational colors of the flowers of these hybrids are truly beautiful to behold and vary much more than those of the true species. Flowering can be manipulated artificially by varying the day length (short days and long nights promote flowering).

Location: This species is perfectly adapted to cultivation in hanging baskets, which allows the observer to view the subtle flowers at eye level.

The flowers are adapted for pollination by birds, while its ability to flower profusely gives it horticultural value. It prefers dappled shade and is sure to become scorched if exposed to direct, bright sunlight for long periods.

Plants are frost-tender and should be protected from harsh winter temperatures. The soil mixture should be well drained, but should not be allowed to dry out completely between waterings. The species will benefit from the addition of fertilizer during the flowering season.

Natural habitat: Indigenous to the Rio de Janeiro province of Brazil.

When viewed from the side, the flowers of *Schlumbergera truncata* are shaped like small birds.

Number of species: Eight species are included in *Stenocactus* (which is also known by various names in the now defunct genus *Echinofossulocactus*).

Common name: Book Cactus, alluding to the thin, wavy, closely packed ribs that resemble the pages of a book.

Description: The pale green stems of this globose cactus are beautifully fluted into numerous thin ribs, which are wavy and carry straight, grayish-white spines on the small areoles.

The flowers are purplish pink and are borne at the slightly depressed apex of the plants. They are produced during the day in midsummer.

Notes: This is a cactus curiosity that warrants cultivation purely for the fascination in its oddity. The ribs are closely packed, creating the impression that the plants have not received water for a considerable period of time. However, this is what the plant looks like even when well fed.

Location: The species is not at all difficult to cultivate, provided care is taken not to overwater it. It requires strong sunlight to look its best.

Country of origin: Northern and central Mexico.

When under water stress, the zigzag, concertina-shaped arrangement of the ribs of the very variable *Stenocactus crispatus* are almost entirely obscured by the dense layer of spines. The flowers, although quite small, are a beautiful shade of soft pink.

Stenocereus eruca (also widely known as Machaerocereus eruca)
Creeping Devil Cactus

Number of species: 24 species are included in *Stenocereus*.

Common name: Creeping Devil Cactus, which refers to the very thorny stems that creep along the ground, with only the terminal portions of the stems turned upward.

Description: The pale, dusty-green stems of this species have multiple ribs and creep along the ground, rooting as they grow. Only the tips of the rather heavy stems tend to be erect, enabling the stems to climb over rocks in their paths. The stems are profusely covered with very sharp, pungent, off-white, dagger-shaped spines that are sure to cause harm to an unsuspecting person treading on them.

The flowers are a pale pinkish to creamish color and open at night.

Notes: The common name of the species is quite appropriate: the rear parts slowly dies off while the new growth of the stems take root.

As with so many cacti, this species is grown for its stems and thorns, rather than its flowers.

In its natural habitat the creeping, rooted stems of the plants play an important ecological role in that they act as effective soil binders. Because of this typical creeping habit, it is sure to be a talking point in any collection.

Location: The species is not all that common in cultivation, probably as a result of its creeping habit. It is therefore not suitable for long-term culture in a pot, unless you use a long narrow box (at least 3 ft./1 m long).

The stout spines are very attractive and it certainly warrants being grown in open beds, where it can make an interesting addition to any collection.

Stem cuttings root easily and the plants require a well-drained sandy soil mixture and a sunny position.

Natural habitat: Baja California Sur in Mexico.

Close-up of the formidable dagger-shaped spines of *Stenocereus eruca*.

The carpet-forming stems of the Mexican Creeping Devil, *Stenocereus eruca*, are armed with short, but formidable spines.

Number of species: 4 species are currently recognized in *Tephrocactus*.

Common name: Paper-Spined Cactus, referring to the long, papery spines of this species.

Description: Plants form erect, but low-growing spreading clumps, consisting of pale green upright or creeping stems. The distinctly jointed stems consist of cylindrical pads that vary from 1½–2 in. (3–6 cm) in length.

The areoles are very large and prominent. They are fringed with short, dark brown glochids, but the plants are often spineless. If spines (thorns) are present, they are rather harmless and papery, but can reach a length of up to 4 in. (10 cm).

The flowers are fairly large and creamy white to pinkish.

Notes: The species is often grown as a curiosity because of its long, papery spines. The ease with which it can be grown makes it a perfect inclusion in a cacti "starter pack" for a beginner. The form of this species with papery thorns is known as *Tephrocactus articulatus* fa. *papyracanthus*.

Location: There are no challenges in cultivating *Tephrocactus articulatus* and it will grow in virtually any type of soil and climate. The ease with which the species can be cultivated carries a message, though, as it quickly becomes naturalized in areas with a climate similar to that which it experiences in its natural habitat.

Be careful not to allow the species to spread into areas where it could become a minor menace.

Natural habitat: Western Argentina.

Not all the forms of *Tephrocactus articulatus* have the extensive papery thorns from which the common name was derived; this one has only a few such thorns.

Trichocereus spachianus
Torch, Golden Torch Cactus

Number of species: About 10 species are currently recognized in *Trichocereus*.

Common name: Torch Cactus, Golden Torch Cactus, or Small Queen of the Night, an indication that the large, white flowers of the species open at night and, in bright moonlight, shine like torches.

Description: The stems of this clump-forming species are typically columnar and up to 6½ ft. (2 m) tall.

The bright green, distinctly ribbed stems tend to get top-heavy and will topple over if they are not supported by tying them to a stake.

The edges of the ribs are neatly adorned with vertical columns of small clumps of very pungent, amber-brown, needlelike spines.

The large, night-opening flowers are white with yellowish outer segments and are borne in midsummer.

Notes: This species is widely cultivated as a hedge or border, as well as a container plant in arid regions.

It grows exceptionally easily, and herein lies a danger: it can easily spread and become a troublesome weed. The species is also referred to as *Echinopsis spachiana*, *Echinopsis schickendantzii*, or *Trichocereus schickendantzii*.

Location: Plants are very easy to cultivate and thrive on neglect and in full sun. However, care should be taken not to allow the species to spread: it can easily escape from domestic gardens and become a pest plant in countries very remote from its natural habitat.

Natural habitat: Western Argentina.

Top. *Trichocereus spachianus* stems are strongly ribbed and carry fairly short, sharp spines. The flower buds are adorned with soft, brown wool.

Right. A large clump of *Trichocereus spachianus* provides the only horticultural embellishment of a simple house in South Africa's Great Karoo, tens of thousands of miles away from its natural South American habitat.

Neobuxbaumia polylopha tower skyward in Monaco's Jardin Exotique.

CACTI AND SUCCULENT COLLECTIONS

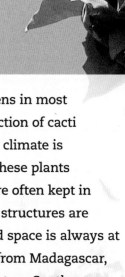

Nowadays, botanical gardens in most major cities include a collection of cacti and succulents. Where the climate is not conducive to growing these plants outdoors, the collections are often kept in conservatories. Since such structures are expensive to maintain, and space is always at a premium, treelike aloes from Madagascar, Mexican agaves, and miniature South African mesembs are often grouped together. Although this is not necessarily a bad thing, it does require a vivid imagination to envision them in an appropriate setting!

There is no doubt that cacti and succulents can best be appreciated in outdoor locations, and enthusiasts should try to visit some of the gardens discussed here.

With literally thousands of species in cultivation, the cactus and succulent plant collection kept in Zürich is widely hailed as one of the most complete in the world. Established many decades ago from a privately donated collection, it has expanded and grown to its present size and, admirably, enjoys the support of the Zürich city fathers.

Most of the plants are kept under glass, with a few of the hardier ones grown in outdoor beds. Given that the Swiss climate is not really conducive to growing succulents outdoors, the keepers of the collection have done well to create small forests of succulents and cacti under glass.

Protecting these sun-loving plants in the outdoor collection from excessive rainfall and destructively low temperatures is a labor-intensive exercise that requires protective covers and lean-to's to be carefully constructed every winter, only to be removed again as the summer approaches.

Visit *www.stadt-zuerich.ch/sukkulenten*.

The shrubby *Agave bracteosa*, a native of Mexico, grows happily in a small space in the Sukkulenten-Sammlung in Zürich, where it is protected by glass from the extremes of the Swiss climate.

Even before this exciting garden impacts on the visitor's senses, the sheer challenge of creating a garden against a vertical cliff face strikes one as a remarkable engineering feat. This wonderful garden and plant collection indeed bears testimony to what can be achieved with sheer willpower and the desire to display the plant wonders of the arid world.

The climate of the French and Italian Rivieras is, without doubt, perfectly suited for the outdoor cultivation of the vast majority of the world's succulents, with hot, dry summers and wet but mild winters.

Having been in existence for about eight decades, and offering a variety of small and large succulents and cacti, this garden is a perfect place to see mature specimens towering over the azure blue of the Mediterranean Sea.

Visit *www.jardin-exotique.mc*.

In the Jardin Exotique one can enjoy striking vistas such as this magnificent specimen of *Beaucarnea recurvata* set against a backdrop of the sparkling Mediterranean Sea.

The Desert Garden, one of 14 themed gardens that comprise the Huntington Library, Art Collection and Botanical Gardens in California, is one of the oldest in the world, although it was established only about a century ago. This gives an idea of just how young succulent plant gardens really are.

Here, in this naturally hot climate, there is no need to keep plants in the lean-to's and cold frames needed in more severe climates. Covering a vast outdoor area, with paths meandering among beds filled with cacti and succulents of all descriptions, the Desert Garden is a perfect setting in which to appreciate the use of these plants in large-scale landscaping.

Visit *www.huntington.org/desertgarden*.

Right. A dense stand of barrel-shaped *Echinocactus grusonii* on display in the Huntington Botanical Gardens.

Opposite page. The near-fluorescent orange flowers of this clump-forming hybrid of *Dyckia fosteriana* brightens up a corner of the Desert Collection.

Desert Botanical Garden

The magnificence of Arizona's Desert Botanical Garden pays tribute to the dedication of a number of far-sighted individuals who were concerned about the destruction of the natural desert environment around Phoenix.

Today, with its extensive outdoor displays open to the public, and its behind-the-scenes collections, the Desert Botanical Garden is a real treasure trove of cacti, succulents, and American southwestern desert flora in general.

As with many botanical gardens, the Desert Garden regularly hosts educational and horticultural training events that inform the public of the benefits of indigenous desert gardening.

Visit *www.dbg.org*.

Right. A magnificent specimen of *Carnegiea gigantea*, the Saguaro Cactus, which is indigenous to the deserts of Arizona, stretches its arms skyward.

Opposite page. A massive specimen of *Pachycereus pringlei* in the Desert Botanical Garden.

CACTI AND SUCCULENTS HANDBOOK

Ganna Walska Lotusland

In Santa Barbara, one of the coastal cities near Los Angeles, small-town charm, yet flair and sophistication abound. It was here in the mild coastal paradise that is California that Madame Ganna Walska established what was to become a world famous Botanical Garden. The magnificently landscaped garden is situated on a stretch of 37 acres (14.9 ha) of fertile, undulating ground: sun-baked California at its best.

If ever there was a garden with character, it is Lotusland, and in many respects it is not constrained by gardening convention. This fascinating and mysterious place that today is covered with mature succulent, semi-tropical and tropical plants is a veritable treasure chest full to the brim with trees, cycads, vines, aquatic plants in lily ponds, and of course masses of succulents that grow in dense profusion in every nook and cranny, at times even hinting at being a jungle. But not in the Amazonian sense, even though even ferns abound. Rather, strange and fat-bodied and fat-leaved plants from around the world grow cheek to jowl in a luxurious and accessible way with the rhythm of the beds soothing on the senses.

From early on Madame Walska had a special interest in creating unusual display gardens that incorporated exotic plants, and this tradition is carried on to this day. While Lotusland contains thousands of different species, the minimalist approach used in some beds makes the Garden timeless. Dense plantings of the same, or similar, cacti, aloes, or agaves place emphasis on shapes, sizes, and textures, of which there are many to play with among succulents.

To visit:

All visits require reservations. Guided tours are offered at 10 and 1:30 from Wednesday to Saturday between mid-February and mid-November. Only 15,000 visitors are allowed per annum to prevent disruption of the tranquillity of the area where it is situated in Montecito, a suburb of Santa Barbara. Visit *visitlotusland.org*.

Some of the most striking horticultural declarations are often made through understatements, and the strongest proclamations are often revealed in attention paid to tiny details. The carefully manicured bed of intensely bluish gray-leaved *Agave franzosinii*, over-topped by furcraeas, additionally creates a sense of serenity in the Blue Garden.

CACTI AND SUCCULENTS HANDBOOK

Is it *Euphorbia ingens*, the naboom of the African savannahs, or *Euphorbia ammak* from the Arabian Peninsula? Regardless, the branches of both species usually grow upright, but those of this world-famous specimen flourishing near the front entrance to the pink-painted stucco villa at Lotusland beguilingly droop and sprawl over the paved path. Although the branches dangle, the specimens themselves stand as tall as the house, so reinforcing the austere integrity of the building.

CACTI AND SUCCULENT COLLECTIONS

111

Originally established at Whitehill near Matjiesfontein in South Africa's Great Karoo, the Karoo Desert National Botanical Garden was relocated in 1946 to its present site in the Worcester-Robertson Karoo, an arid inland region, surrounded by high mountains, some 95 miles (150 km) from Cape Town.

This inland area receives winter rainfall, but much less than the seaward side of the mountains. As with all South Africa's national botanical gardens, the plants cultivated in the Karoo Desert Garden originate from within the country, which has the richest diversity of succulents globally, with over 4,500 species recorded.

Apart from immaculately kept collections of southern African succulent plant groups, such as *Haworthia* and its generic relatives, the garden features the largest man-made forest of quiver trees (*Aloidendron dichotomum*) in the world, a useful plants section, and a maze planted exclusively with Pork Bush (*Portulacaria afra*).

In a large landscape, such as here in the Karoo Desert National Botanical Garden, aloes combine well with many other succulents, including the low-growing *Kalanchoe thyrsiflora* (red leaves; middle ground).

CACTI AND SUCCULENTS HANDBOOK

Kirstenbosch National Botanical Garden

Kirstenbosch National Botanical Garden in Cape Town consists of a series of sections and beds that are dedicated to specific plant groups, rather than to plants from particular countries.

Kirstenbosch is the flagship of the National Botanical Gardens, which are managed by the South African National Biodiversity Institute (SANBI).

The garden grows indigenous South African material only but, being at the heart of the botanically diverse Cape Floral Kingdom, and with the richest temperate flora in the world present in South Africa, there is a vast range of material to choose from.

The Western Cape is situated in a winter rainfall area, so those succulent species that will not survive outdoors are displayed under glass in the Botanical Society Conservatory.

In the early years of Kirstenbosch's development, drainage was improved in a section of the garden that eventually became the Matthews Rockery, which now accommodates large and mature succulent plant specimens in open beds without the fear that the plants will succumb to the high rainfall.

The roof crossbeams cast a network of rectangular shadows over the plants on display in the Botanical Society Conservatory at Kirstenbosch.

CACTI and SUCCULENTS HANDBOOK

The near black-leaved *Aeonium arboreum* 'Zwartkop' is a member of the family Crassulaceae.

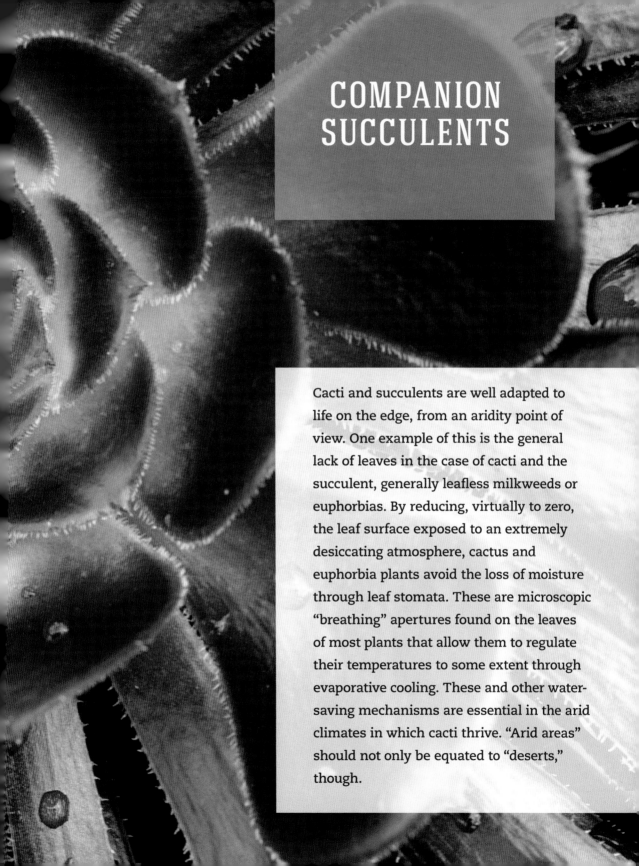

COMPANION SUCCULENTS

Cacti and succulents are well adapted to life on the edge, from an aridity point of view. One example of this is the general lack of leaves in the case of cacti and the succulent, generally leafless milkweeds or euphorbias. By reducing, virtually to zero, the leaf surface exposed to an extremely desiccating atmosphere, cactus and euphorbia plants avoid the loss of moisture through leaf stomata. These are microscopic "breathing" apertures found on the leaves of most plants that allow them to regulate their temperatures to some extent through evaporative cooling. These and other water-saving mechanisms are essential in the arid climates in which cacti thrive. "Arid areas" should not only be equated to "deserts," though.

Agave americana subsp. *americana* var. *marginata*

AGAVACEAE

Representatives of the Agavaceae are mostly leaf succulents that have their leaves arranged in strong rosettes. Species of *Agave* are generally known as century plants. This is an allusion to the fact that they generally take many years, in rare cases 15 to 20 or more, to reach flowering maturity.

Most species of *Agave* are very easy to cultivate and make excellent companions for cacti. As a general rule, agaves are monocarpic. This means that they grow for many years and then flower once before dying.

Apart from producing copious amounts of seed, many agaves also produce bulbils (perfectly formed plantlets) on their inflorescences. These root easily and can be planted to ensure the next generation of that species in a garden.

Most species of the family are remarkably hardy and will easily survive in dry, cold winter conditions. Under colder climatic conditions, *Agave* should be protected from growing media that are waterlogged in winter. Species originating from tropical areas such as the Caribbean islands will, however, show varying degrees of leaf damage at temperatures below 32°F (0°C).

Representatives of a number of other agavoid genera are common in cultivation in many parts of the world. Some of these are discussed here.

Like so many cacti, they also originate from the New World, particularly Mexico and the southern USA. Some species, for example *Agave americana* and *Agave sisalana*, sucker excessively and care should be taken that they are not planted too close to prized cacti as they will very rapidly smother them.

It has been suggested that the Agavaceae should be included in the Asparagaceae, but we here retain it as a family in its own right.

The architectural blue leaves of *Agave americana* subsp. *americana* will enhance the greenery of associated cactus plants.

The soft leaved *Agave attenuata* is perfect for cultivaton in subtropical areas. with a mild climate.

Agave americana subsp. *americana*

The common name of this species, which originates from Mexico, is "century plant," referring to the very long time it takes to flower.

The leaves are sword-shaped, with a distinct blueish color. They are arranged in large basal rosettes that can be over 3 ft. (1 m) in diameter. The leaf margins are armed with vicious spines. After about 12 years, mature plants produce a massive, towering flowering pole, resembling a lightning conductor.

The flowers are greenish yellow and have a strong fruity smell.

The species produces an embarrassment of sideshoots from ground level, but hardly ever any bulbils on the inflorescence pole.

The species is exceedingly adaptable to a variety of growing conditions and will tolerate extreme drought, tropical rain conditions, sweltering heat, and freezing cold. Indeed, this is one of the few succulent plants of which it can be claimed that it will grow and thrive virtually anywhere. Propagation is from the many basal sprouts it produces, even as a young, immature plant.

Agave attenuata

Plants grow as medium-sized shrubs to small single-trunked trees that carry large rosettes at the ends of the stems. The leaves are very soft and pliable, in contrast to those of most species of Agave. The leaf margins and both leaf surfaces are smooth and devoid of any spines. The leaves stiffen and twirl as they dry and are easily shed, exposing a smooth, clean stem.

The inflorescence grows vertically at first, after which it gracefully curves outward in the shape of the trunk of an elephant. The large flowers are a light green color.

The species hails from Mexico, but is now found all over the world. It is a wonderful landscape plant for tropical and subtropical gardens, but the leaves are easily damaged by harsh climates and subzero temperatures.

Agave mitis var. *albidior* is proliferous. If planted against a slope, its blue rosettes resemble a cascading waterfall.

The leaf margins of *Agave filifera* are adorned with threadlike appendages.

A plant of Mexican origin, *Agave filifera* has striking purple flowers. It can withstand a wide range of temperatures.

Agave mitis var. albidior

Plants grow as robust, multiheaded shrubs, with medium-sized rosettes tightly packed in a clump. The leaves are light green to blueish white, and the margins have small, brown teeth.

After six to eight years, a robust, unbranched inflorescence appears from the center of a rosette. The flowers are fairly large and green, tinged with red. The tips of the floral segments are strongly recurved, giving the inflorescence an almost fluffy appearance.

When clumps of this Mexican species mature, it seems that, at any time, at least one rosette is producing an inflorescence. (Only the rosette that produces an inflorescence dies. The rest of the clump keeps growing.)

The best horticultural feature is the neat, open rosettes that in time form dense stands. Their clumping habit means that once a rosette has flowered and starts to wither, it is rapidly replaced by another, so that gaps do not develop in the greenery.

Agave filifera

Plants grow as medium-sized rosettes that sucker prolifically from the base. The leaves are light green and very sharply tipped. Both leaf surfaces are adorned with longitudinal white bands and marginal threads haphazardly curl away from the leaf margins.

A tall, unbranched inflorescence is produced after many years. Large, purplish green flowers are carried on short stalks along the upper two thirds of an inflorescence.

A useful agave for landscaping, as it takes up to 18 years to reach flowering age, while it slowly increases in size to form large clumps of more or less ball-shaped rosettes. Propagation is almost exclusively from the side shoots it produces.

The leaves of *Agave geminiflora* are thin and pliable and adorned with white marginal threads.

With its smooth leaf margins, *Agave sisalana* is quite decorative, especially if contrasted against white gravel.

Agave geminiflora

Plants grow as single, unbranched, medium-sized rosettes. The leaves are bright green, fairly thin, and pliable and their margins are beautifully adorned with short, white threads. (The leaves of some forms lack the white threads, but the most desirable ones to grow are those with prominent marginal threads.) The set of young leaves in the center of a rosette are tightly packed into a compact cone.

After many years of growth, a single, unbranched flowering pole is produced. The flowers, borne in small clusters, are greenish, tinged with red.

This noninvasive Mexican species does not form plantlets from the base. Propagation is through seed that germinates easily.

Agave sisalana

Plants grow as medium-sized to large rosettes that produce many suckers from the base. The deep green leaves generally lack marginal spines.

After several years a massive, much-branched flowering pole is produced. The flowers are green and carried vertically on the side branches of the inflorescence. There is no seed, but thousands of plantlets are formed on the inflorescence.

As is often the case with agricultural crops, the Mexican *Agave sisalana* (sisal) has variable forms. The most popular horticultural forms have variegated leaves with white, longitudinal sections.

In parts of the world, *Agave sisalana* is grown in plantations, as the leaf fibers are used to produce ropes and mats.

Plants of *Agave lechuiguilla* form small to medium-sized rosettes that produce a profusion of basal suckers.

The flowering of *Agave salmiana* is a significant event as it sends a massive flowering pole skyward.

Agave lechuiguilla

Plants grow as small to medium-sized rosettes that rapidly produce a profusion of suckers. The leaves are fairly narrow and adorned with very sharp marginal teeth. Leaf color varies somewhat, but the most commonly cultivated forms have light green to yellowish green leaves.

After years of vegetative growth, a single, unbranched inflorescence is produced that carries ball-shaped clusters of yellow flowers that are tinged with red.

This is a very variable Mexican species and not all the forms are horticulturally successful. However, it is immensely hardy and will thrive in virtually any soil type and position.

As is the case with many species of Agave, it produces a profusion of suckers that should be trimmed off if a single rosette is desired.

The fibers of this species' leaves are very tough and have been used for the production of rope.

Agave salmiana var. salmiana

Plants grow as massive, open rosettes that slowly sucker from the base. The leaves are narrow toward their bases and then rapidly broaden toward their middle parts, before terminating in a long, menacingly sharp spine. The leaf margins carry very pungent spines that are sure to cause discomfort to unobservant passers-by, should they inadvertently bump into them.

After several years, typically more than 10, a massive inflorescence with horizontal side branches will appear from the center of a rosette. These branches carry dense, flat-topped clusters of dark greenish yellow flowers that are sometimes replaced by small plantlets that can be easily rooted to start a new generation.

The ideal position for this majestic plant is as a centerpiece in a bed that contains nothing but a few plants of the species. The soil should be covered with gravel of a contrasting color and the emerging suckers should be removed to allow a plant to more rapidly grow to maturity.

To this day, this dull green leaved species is used as one of the primary sources of pulque, a fermented drink produced in Mexico from the plant sap that accumulates in the center of a rosette of which the central portion has been removed.

Agave victoria-reginae

These are small to medium-sized plants (at least for Agave), with tightly packed, very neat rosettes. These are typically ball-shaped, which gives them a pleasing appearance as their shape emulates that of some of the larger globular or barrel-shaped cacti.

The leaves are generally fairly short and stubby with very sharp terminal spikes. The densely arranged leaves are striking, in that they are adorned with distinct white lines, or bud imprints, on both surfaces.

At maturity the plant produces a single unbranched, sturdy, robust inflorescence that hardly seems compatible with the comparatively small rosettes.

This species, which was named for Britain's Queen Victoria, is indigenous to Mexico. It is a most desirable plant to have in a collection.

Some of the forms of *Agave victoria-reginae* sucker freely, while others will remain as single rosettes.

In some forms of the species, the white lines on the leaves are rather faint. Understandably, the most popular forms among collectors are those that have their leaves adorned with robust white lines.

The rosettes of *Agave victoria-reginae* consist of short stubby leaves that are densely packed in a tight rosette.

These plants are striking in any setting, with or without cacti. Care should be taken that plants are not overwatered; they succumb easily to fungal rot if the soil in which they grow is kept wet for prolonged periods.

ABOUT AGAVES

Species of the horticulturally useful genus *Agave* are generally referred to as century plants because they take many years to flower—but certainly not a hundred years! Even the most long-lived of the agaves will flower more or less within 15–20 years. Once they have flowered, they die, leaving seed that will rapidly germinate, or they sprout plantlets, either at the base of the plant or on the inflorescence. The plants formed in the latter way are called bulbils and are perfect miniatures of the mature mother plant.

Although the flowers of *Beschorneria yuccoides* are a greenish color, the inflorescence and flower stalks are red.

The variegated form of *Furcraea foetida*, known as cultivar *medio-picta*, displayed against a backdrop of *Yucca aloifolia*.

Beschorneria yuccoides

Plants grow as medium-sized to large, stemless shrubs with numerous soft leaves. The leaves are a blueish green color, soft and pliable, and have a sandpapery texture. The leaf margins lack prominent spines, but they are finely sawtoothed.

The inflorescence is quite large and robust and tends to droop from the vertical. It carries large flowers widely spaced around the central stalk. The flowers are greenish yellow, but the bracts are a striking red color.

This Mexican native is remarkably cold and drought tolerant, and subzero temperatures do it no harm at all.

Unlike the leaves of most *Agave* species, those of *Beschorneria* are soft and they do not carry sharp spines.

Furcraea foetida

Plants grow as large, clump-forming specimens. Individual rosettes can reach massive proportions that make the plants somewhat resemble small palm trees. The leaves are bright green and slightly rough to the touch. The leaf margins are smooth with only a few small, scattered teeth toward the lower parts of the leaves.

After about 15 years of growth, a massive, much-branched inflorescence is produced, with greenish white flowers hanging down from the side branches. Small plantlets that are at first globular in shape are carried on the inflorescence branches.

By far the most desirable form of the species to grow is the variety known as medio-picta, that has broad, white central sections to the leaves.

It also grows much more slowly than other varieties, and is smaller, making it a more manageable plant in a domestic garden.

Neither the pure species, nor the cultivar (horticultural variant) can tolerate low temperatures.

The normal form of *Furcraea foetida*, which derives from the northern parts of South America, is an aggressive grower that can easily become invasive, especially in subtropical regions.

In a healthy clump of *Hesperaloe parviflora* plants, the leaves form a tangled mass. The leaves have short, curled, white threadlike filaments on their margins. These plants do well in the open ground or in containers.

Manfreda maculosa will rapidly spread in a bed to form rosulate clumps of highly colored leaves.

Hesperaloe parviflora

Plants grow as small to medium-sized clumps of slender-leaved rosettes. The leaves vary from dark to blueish green, with indistinct longitudinal lines on both surfaces. The leaf margins carry beautifully curled thread-like filaments.

A tall, branched inflorescence is produced in early to midsummer. Small clusters of open, Aloe-like flowers, varying from dull pink to deep, bright red, are carried on the inflorescence. After successful fertilization of the flowers, fat, bright green capsules filled with large, black seeds are produced.

Hesperaloe parviflora is native to northern Mexico and southwestern USA. The species shows considerable variation in its leaf and inflorescence characters. The latter can be tall and drooping, unable to support its own weight, or short and erect.

Propagation is through the division of clumps, or easily germinated seed.

Manfreda maculosa
(sometimes treated as *Agave maculosa*)

Plants grow as low mats, like ground cover. They consist of small rosettes of fairly long, soft, floppy leaves that are deeply channeled. The leaves are uniformly dull green or have large, purplish brown blotches, particularly on the upper surfaces, and the leaf margins are finely sawtoothed.

The inflorescence is very long and carries large, open-mouthed flowers in a sparse arrangement. The flower buds are a muted green, while the open, reflexed floral parts are a golden brownish color.

This species originates from Mexico and the southern USA. Plants are deciduous, which means they die back to ground level during the winter months. In spring the leaves reemerge with fresh vigor.

The easiest way to propagate this species is by dividing existing clumps.

The leaves are quite brittle and can be easily damaged by pedestrian traffic alongside a bed in which plants have been established.

The reflexed portions of the flower parts of *Manfreda maculosa* are golden brown.

Yucca aloifolia stems sometimes require support to keep them erect. Otherwise they tend to sprawl along the ground. In very cold or very hot weather the leaf tips take on a reddish tinge. The waxy white flowers (above) are lantern-shaped.

The leaf margins of *Yucca carnerosana* are adorned with white, threadlike filaments.

YUCCA

Yucca aloifolia

Plants grow as robust, multistemmed shrubs. The stems are covered with stiff, spreading leaves that take quite a while to dry out. Once dry, the leaves turn down vertically to effectively clothe the stem. The leaves are dull green, very sharp-tipped and have margins that are sawtoothed. The many-branched inflorescence has large, white lantern-shaped flowers.

The stems of this Mexican species require support, otherwise they typically topple over and sprawl along the ground.

The dried, and even the green, leaves of *Yucca aloifolia* can be safely removed without the risk of harm to the plants, resulting in plants with a clean, neat appearance.

This is one of the fastest growing yuccas available in cultivation. Many other species require quite some time to reach flowering maturity.

Yucca carnerosana

Plants typically grow as robust, single stemmed specimens. The leaves are borne erectly to form a stiff rosette. The leaves are a deep green color and the leaf margins are adorned with a multitude of grayish white threads. The dried leaves remain attached to the plant for a long time and bend down vertically to almost completely cover the trunk.

The much-branched inflorescence carries dense clusters of white flowers.

The species is indigenous to northwestern Mexico and some parts of the southeastern USA.

The robust growth form of the species makes it very desirable to have growing in a garden, although it is not very hardy in cold climates.

ABOUT YUCCAS

Species of the predominantly Mexican genus *Yucca* are extremely frost-hardy. Most of them will easily tolerate temperatures of well below freezing point without showing even the slightest sign of damage, and will therefore provide beautiful greenery even during some of the severest winters experienced in the temperate and central-continental parts of the world.

Mexico's *Yucca guatemalensis* has very strong, erect stems that will eventually tower over companion plants.

The variegated leaves of the cultivar 'Golden Sword' of *Yucca filamentosa* shimmer golden in the sunlight.

Yucca guatemalensis

Plants grow as clusters of branches arising from a swollen base. The trunks are covered by long, dagger-shaped green leaves with sharp, but harmless, tips. The leaves stay attached to the plants for a long time.

The much-branched inflorescence is fairly short. The bell-shaped flowers are bright white and quite large. Plants take a long time to flower.

This species, one of the most widely cultivated stem succulents, thrives in subtropical regions, but is also both cold hardy and drought tolerant. It can be propagated through stem cuttings.

One of the most desirable forms has leaves with yellow margins. Older leaves are easily removed, without detriment to the plant, to expose the architectural stems.

Yucca filamentosa

Plants grow as low, usually stemless, shrubs that consist of basal rosettes. The leaves are narrow and only slightly succulent. The leaf margins are adorned with long, white threadlike filaments.

The flowers are quite large, bright white, and waxy.

This species, from the eastern parts of the USA, is exceptionally hardy. It can tolerate dry, desertlike conditions, very high and very low temperatures, and even considerable overwatering.

The horticulturally most useful form of the species is the one whose leaves have a prominent central yellow stripe.

Lampranthus glaucus

AIZOACEAE

The members of this, the largest of the world's succulent plant families, are fascinating in all respects. The family includes about 1,800 species; about as many cacti are recognized globally. While the cacti are mostly restricted to the New World, most aizooids that appeal to collectors are restricted to South Africa's western winter-rainfall area. They are typically leaf succulents, but some also have thick, swollen stems and/or roots. Furthermore, they show exceptional variation in terms of growth forms, ranging from tiny, water-filled plant bodies to small, much-branched trees.

The azooids, which are here interchangeably also referred to as mesembs, are still sometimes treated as belonging to the family Mesembryanthemaceae. Here a broader family concept is followed that includes the Mesembryanthemaceae, and a few other families, in the more inclusive Aizoaceae.

The flowers of the mesembs superficially resemble the head-shaped inflorescences of daisy plants. The fruits are interesting in that they open and close in response to moisture. When they get wet, during a downpour for example, seeds are dislodged from the fruit capsules, which close again once the rain stops, only to reopen during the next rain shower.

Two groups of mesembs are particularly popular among succulent plant collectors: the representatives with pebble-shaped bodies (*Lithops* spp.), and the shrubs with brightly colored flowers, such as *Lampranthus* and *Ruschia* species.

In their natural habitats, the shrubby plants are often insignificant-looking, rather scraggly plants, but in cultivation they form nicely rounded canopies that are covered in flowers that can be virtually any color except blue and black!

In contrast, the plant bodies of the pebble plants, which are often two-leaved, are sunk into the ground in their habitats but, in cultivation, will rapidly take on a rather unnatural appearance as they respond to an abundance of water and comparatively low light intensities.

In warm climates, the shrubs should be planted out in the open where they are protected against too much water and very low temperatures. The stone plants often do much better in pots, where the amount of water they receive can be carefully controlled. In general, the mesembs are not very hardy in cold climates, as most species have soft leaves that are easily damaged by frost. Plants must be protected against frost and, especially those that originate in summer rainfall areas, from winter rain coupled with subzero temperatures.

Ebracteola wilmaniae has green, fingerlike leaves dotted with dark spots. The flowers are pinkish purple with white sections.

Lampranthus glaucus produces an array of butter yellow flowers in the spring months.

Ebracteola wilmaniae

Plants grow as very low clumps that have numerous finger-like leaves exposed above ground.

The leaves are soft, and a pleasant sea green color, tinged with purplish pink, with numerous tiny, darker spots dotted all over them. The flowers are a light pink color, with white centers.

The species is indigenous to South Africa's interior savanna and grassland areas. In its natural habitat it is often found in the rather thin clay soils in rock depressions.

Ebracteola wilmaniae is propagated through division of the clumps. Seeds also germinate without difficulty. It prefers summer rain, and can tolerate a surprising amount of it if planted in open beds with good drainage.

Lampranthus glaucus

Plants grow as small, manageable shrublets. The stems are thin and soft, especially when young. The slightly angled, cylindrical leaves are short with blunt tips and carried some distance apart on the purplish green stems.

The flowers are quite large and bright yellow. These are borne in profusion in spring.

The species is indigenous to coastal and adjacent inland parts of South Africa's Western Cape.

Plants remain as small shrublets but, if planted closely together, will form a continuous mat, producing an amazing display of golden yellow flowers.

When fully expanded, the bright yellow flowers of *Lithops lesliei* subsp. *lesliei* completely obscure the plant body.

Ruschia intricata produces a myriad bright purple flowers in the summer months. The stems carry sharp spines.

Lithops lesliei subsp. *lesliei*

These small, button-shaped stone plants resemble the pebbles among which they grow. The plant bodies consist of two leaves that are fused basally, usually below ground level, with only the flattened tips exposed.

The visible leaf tips have interesting patterns and light-colored windows, giving rise to the common name, Window Plants, which is sometimes applied to many different mesembs.

The bright yellow flowers are quite large. The plants become visible only once the flowers close at night, or during inclement weather.

Lithops lesliei has a preference for summer rainfall. It is widely distributed in the grasslands and adjacent areas of the South African interior.

Unlike many *Mesembryanthemaceae*, it does not mind clay soil. However, plants should not be left in wet, poorly drained soil for long periods.

A fascination with the strange shape, size, and outline of *Lithops* species is often the reason why people start succulent plant collections.

Ruschia intricata

Plants grow as medium-sized, rounded shrubs that consist of thin, stiff, somewhat woody stems and branches.

The leaves are very much reduced and cylindrical and the flowers are a striking, bright purple color.

Rushia intricata, previously and widely known as *Eberlanzia spinosa*, is indigenous to the central karroid and grassland regions of South Africa.

Thorns are not the main defense mechanism used by most mesemb species. However, *Ruschia intricata* has exceptionally sharp, stiff thorns that are sure to cause discomfort to an unobservant passerby.

This species is exceptionally cold hardy, and subzero temperatures do it no harm whatsoever.

CACTI AND SUCCULENTS HANDBOOK

APOCYNACEAE

Stapelia gigantea

The inclusion of the well-known carrion flower family, the Asclepiadaceae, in the more diverse, and now much larger, family Apocynaceae is nowadays widely accepted. The genus *Stapelia*, the name of which has become accepted as a common name for many representatives of the family, as stapeliads, is perhaps the best known of the carrion flower genera. The stapeliads and their numerous generic relatives are essentially stem succulents with smooth or hairy surfaces, but some, at least, also have succulent leaves (e.g., representatives of *Ceropegia*) and/or caudices (e.g., representatives of *Brachystelma*).

Few succulent plants can boast such intriguing flowers as characterize the stapeliads, whose internal and external surfaces often sport small, tendril-like appendages that will break into motion at the slightest breeze, emulating fungal threads. The flowers often appear oversized for the fairly small size of the plants and many are in muted shades of russet and purple. In addition to the intricacies of the flowers' structure, the succulent representatives of the family have a further claim to fame: their flowers smell like decaying meat. They are adapted for insect pollination, which is often performed by bluebottles (blowflies) and house flies.

Most representatives of the family Apocynaceae occur naturally in temperate regions that experience either summer or winter rainfall in fairly limited amounts. However, none of these regions are subjected to the severely cold, wet conditions prevalent in colder climates. They should therefore be kept in heated (ideally) or unheated (risky) greenhouses.

Apart from the stapeliads, the Apocynaceae, quite a large plant family as presently circumscribed, includes species that used to be classified on their own in this family, such as *Adenium*. As a further example, the frangipanis, with their sweet-smelling flowers, are included in this subdivision of the Apocynaceae.

Hoodia pilifera subsp. annulata

Plants grow as large clumps of cactus-like stems. The stems are a grayish white color, leafless and covered with spine-like protuberances.

The flowers are a deep chocolate brown color and quite large.

It is best to grow the species from seed as stem cuttings do not root that easily.

The species is very particular as far as watering is concerned and care should be taken not to overwater plants in cultivation.

This species is indigenous to South Africa's arid interior, particularly the karroid regions.

Orbea lutea subsp. lutea

Plants grow as small clumps of creeping stems that can cover quite large areas. The angled stems carry numerous harmless, spinelike protuberances on their margins. The flowers, produced in small clusters, are mostly uniformly yellow, and foul-smelling.

The species has a wide geographical distribution, and occurs naturally in South Africa's interior savanna region.

Orbea lutea subsp. *lutea* is easy to cultivate from stem cuttings. The plants often creep along the ground toward suitable microenvoronments where they can flourish, such as a shady corner under surrounding plants.

This species produces some of the strongest smelling flowers of all the asclepiads.

The erect stems of *Hoodia pilifera* subsp. *annulata* closely resemble those of cactus plants. During the flowering season, they are covered with chocolate brown flowers.

The bright yellow, foul-smelling flowers of *Orbea lutea* subsp. *lutea* are borne in small clusters near the tips of the stems.

The flowers of this cultivar of *Plumeria rubra* are a pleasant mixture of creamy yellow and pink.

In the summer months, *Stapelia gigantea* produces numerous very large flowers that are the color of rotting meat.

Plumeria rubra

Plants grow as medium-sized to very large trees. The stems are fairly thin and smooth. The leaves are shiny green and distinctly shield-shaped.

The flowers of this Mesoamerican species are trumpet-shaped and vary considerably in color. They must rate as some of the most desirable among all the succulent trees. Although *Plumeria rubra* trees drop their leaves in winter, the fragrant flowers make up for any irritation caused by collecting the fallen leaves.

The plants are typically tropical and will create a truly splendid show in summer in any garden. In tropical and subtropical climates, trees grow very quickly and may require pruning from time to time.

Stapelia gigantea

Plants grow as clumps of short, erect, fingerlike stems, which are velvety and angled. Short, stubby protuberances occur along the edges of the angles.

The flowers are a deep brick red color and are produced throughout the hot summer months.

The species is indigenous to South Africa's savanna interior, where they grow under the protection of rocks and bushes. Seed germination is profuse, but stem cuttings, which root easily, are the preferred method of propagation.

This is arguably the most widely grown of all the carrion flowers. The flowers are very large; in fact they are the largest single flowers encountered among succulent plants globally.

ASPHODELACEAE

All representatives of the subfamily Alooideae of the Asphodelaceae, (sometimes accorded family status as the Aloaceae), have succulent leaves variously arranged into rosettes. Indeed, aloes have a growth form not unlike that of agaves, but they are long-lived perennials that will flower regularly year after year, once they have reached reproductive maturity.

With the exception of representatives of the genera *Haworthia*, *Haworthiopsis*, *Tulista*, and *Astroloba*, their flowers are brightly colored, and many species bear a succession of red, orange, or yellow torches during a single flowering season. They tend to flower in winter when many of their companion plants are in a drab, resting phase.

Depending on the preferred classification, the *Aloe* subfamily consists of up to 11 genera. The aloes and their close relatives are nowadays arranged into the following genera: *Aloe* (true aloes), *Aloidendron* (tree aloes), *Kumara* (fan aloes), *Aloiampelos* (rambling aloes), *Aristaloe* (awn-leaf aloe), *Gonialoe* (*kanniedood* aloes), *Gasteria* (gasterias), *Astroloba* (astrolobas), *Haworthia* (haworthias), *Haworthiopsis* (angled haworthias), and *Tulista* (robust haworthias). However, the species most widely cultivated belong to three major genera: *Aloe*, *Haworthia*, and *Gasteria*. Most representatives of this family are easily damaged by subzero temperatures. They will certainly require protection against frosty conditions, especially if grown in areas that receive excessive rainfall.

Flowers of *Gasteria* species are about the size of those of most *Aloe* species, but they tend to be curved and shaped like small bananas. Perhaps, most characteristically, the flowers of the majority of the species have a basal, bulb-like swelling. Their leaves are often tongue-shaped, and the leaf margins armed with a horny edge.

In contrast, representatives of *Haworthia* and its generic relatives have small, mostly nondescript, muted white flowers, and small rosettes of *Aloe*-like leaves. The fascinating leaf shapes and textures of *Haworthia* species are major reasons for their popularity among succulent plant collectors.

The other subfamily of the Asphodelaceae, the Asphodeloideae, includes the red hot pokers (*Kniphofia* species), representatives of which prefer moist habitats. Only some genera of this group, such as *Bulbine*, have fat, water-filled leaves.

Aloes are known for bright colored inflorescences of densely or laxly arranged tubular flowers, such as this natural hybrid between *Aloe ferox* and *Aloe africana*.

Aloe arborescens, a perennial favorite, produces a profusion of brightly colored inflorescences during the winter, although summer-flowering forms are known.

Aloe castanea inflorescences are long and curved with a striking resemblance to a cat's quivering tail, giving rise to the common name, Cat's Tail Aloe.

Aloe arborescens

These much-branched, robust shrubs consist of numerous rosettes carried on stems clothed in the remains of dried leaves. The leaves are generally sickle-shaped, with short, stout but fairly harmless teeth.

Each rosette bears one or more inflorescences, the shape of inverted cones, and consisting of pencil-shaped flowers that vary from red through orange to yellow.

The stems and rosettes tend to be tightly packed, resulting in a beautiful, rounded plant with a neat appearance, that can be planted almost anywhere in a garden, or in a container.

The wide distribution range, from coastal dunes to high altitude, indicates that selected forms will flourish in many different climates.

Aloe castanea

Plants grow as medium-sized trees, most commonly having one or two branches. With age, the stems become smooth, with the remains of dry leaves restricted to the upper parts of the terminal branches.

The dull, matt green leaves are armed with short, sharp teeth along their margins.

The inflorescences are very long and gracefully curved. The small flowers, with their wide mouths, are tightly packed on an inflorescence. Their nectar is a dark chestnut brown.

Aloes are common in the African bushveld or savanna, and few species are more reminiscent of this natural habitat than *Aloe castanea*.

Plants are cold and drought tolerant, but do best in summer rainfall regions.

Aloe comptonii is an ideal plant to grow against a near-vertical cliff face or a dry rock wall in a flowerbed.

The inflorescences of *Aloe ferox* are multibranched and arranged in a candelabra-like fashion.

Aloe comptonii

Plants grow as single or, rarely, doublebranched erect or creeping individuals. The leaves are incurved and a dull blueish-green color. The remains of the old, dry leaves tend to cover most of the stems. The teeth on the leaf margins are short, stout, and distinctly white in color.

The species has a fairly long flowering season in late winter and early spring. The flowers are quite long and carried in distinctly head-shaped inflorescences.

Aloe comptonii inhabits the mountains and rocky outcrops in South Africa's Little Karoo, an arid region in the central-south of the country.

With its short, creeping stems, the species is well adapted to growing against rock faces. In addition, it has few rivals if it is spring color that is desired in a garden.

Horticulturally, the species does equally well in warmer regions that receive winter and summer rain.

Aloe ferox

Plants grow as robust, single-stemmed specimens that carry a single, large rosette. The stems are typically clothed in skirts of dry, boat-shaped leaves with strong teeth on the margins. Some forms, especially those that occur in the Western Cape of South Africa, also have teeth on both leaf surfaces.

The inflorescences are multibranched. The flowers, which range in color from pure white through orange and yellow to bright red, are tightly packed in the strikingly beautiful, torch-like inflorescences, which are borne in winter when few other plants are in flower.

Plants are exceptionally drought tolerant and also able to withstand low, dry temperatures. The skirt of dry leaves should not be removed from cultivated specimens, as it makes for much more natural-looking plants if the leaves are retained.

Extracts of the thick, juice-filled *Aloe ferox* leaves are used in health drinks, skin lotions and shampoos.

Aloe lineata var. *lineata*, which forms large multistemmed, bushy plants, is a perfect aloe to grow in coastal gardens.

Aloe maculata's wide distribution range extends from South Africa's Western Cape to Zimbabwe and beyond.

Aloe lineata var. lineata

Plants often grow as multistemmed clusters, with plantlets and secondary branches clustered along the stem.

The leaves are narrow and sword-shaped, with distinct reddish longitudinal lines. Both upper and lower surfaces are smooth and dull green, and the margins are armed with sharp teeth.

The inflorescences appear blunt-tipped as a result of the long floral leaves that protect the buds. The fairly long flowers vary in color from deep orange to dull pinkish orange.

The species thrives in protected pockets of subtropical thicket in South Africa's Eastern Cape, from sea level to somewhat inland. In cultivation it does very well in both summer and winter rainfall areas.

Aloe maculata

Plants grow as small to medium-sized rosettes; either singly or arranged in multiheaded clusters. The leaves are mostly short and deltoid, and the margins have short, sharp teeth. Both surfaces are mottled with light green to whitish flecks in the shape of an "H."

The flowers have very distinct ball-shaped swellings at the base, and are carried in flat-topped inflorescences.

This species has one of the widest natural distribution ranges of all Aloe species, transcending the boundaries of southern Africa's summer and winter rainfall regions, and confirming its usefulness as a horticultural subject in virtually any setting.

Flowering is variable, with plants flowering throughout the seasons.

Aloe marlothii, a typical savanna species, grows as a single, inbranched plant supporting masssive rosettes on stems skirted by dried leaves.

Aloe peglerae's small, ball-shaped rosettes support short, stout strikingly beautiful inflorescences in the spring.

Aloe marlothii

Plants grow as large, single-stemmed specimens with a robust rosette at the top of a stem clothed in the remains of dead leaves. The large, boat-shaped leaves have teeth along their margins and, most commonly, on both surfaces.

The multibranched inflorescences are carried horizontally. The tubular flowers, borne vertically, vary in color, being uniformly bright red, orange, or bi-colored (orange-yellow; red-white).

This is a typical savanna species of the southern Africa interior. In some parts of its natural distribution range it is exceedingly common and, when in flower, lights up the hillsides with its striking colors. It is a summer rainfall species that can last an entire winter with very little rain.

Aloe peglerae

Plants grow as solitary, small to medium-sized, ball-shaped rosettes. The blueish-green leaves are sickle-shaped and incurved. The leaf margins are densely toothed, while the surfaces may also carry scattered teeth.

The inflorescences are carried on very short stalks that hardly protrude above the rosettes, giving the inflorescences the appearance of rockets being launched from blue globes!

The species originates from a small part of South Africa's savanna grasslands, above the climatically severe inland escarpment.

As a result of the plants' beauty, *Aloe peglerae* has been targeted by illegal collectors for some time. This has resulted in an alarming decline in the number of plants remaining in their natural habitat.

The upper parts of *Aloe pluridens* stems are clothed in the remains of dried leaves; and the rosettes are tilted to one side.

Aloe pratensis occurs naturally in some of the coldest parts of southern Africa, usually favoring rocky outcrops amid the grasslands.

Aloe pluridens

Plants have tall stems that are clothed in the remains of dry, dead, papery leaves for their upper thirds. The rosettes are always tilted to one side and consist of leaves that are distinctly spirally arranged. The leaves are sickle-shaped and light green with indistinct longitudinal striations.

The inflorescences are cone-shaped, like those of *Aloe arborescens*, and consist of long, pencil-shaped flowers. Two color variants, orange (most common) and yellow, are known.

The preferred habitat of *Aloe pluridens* is the dense, almost impenetrable thicket vegetation of South Africa's Eastern Cape province.

Plants of this aloe should ideally be planted among other plants, with only its crown visible. It thrives in filtered and direct sunlight, but cannot tolerate temperature extremes.

Aloe pratensis

Plants grow as small, stemless, open rosettes. The leaves are a striking blueish green color, and the leaf margins and leaf surfaces are adorned with stout teeth.

The compact growth form and robust inflorescence of this aloe have contributed to its popularity among collectors, resulting in plants being removed illegally from their natural habitats. Sadly, the species does not transplant well and wild collected material almost invariably dies an agonizingly slow death in cultivation.

The species grows naturally in the Eastern Cape grassland areas. Its distribution range includes some of the coldest parts of southern Africa, including the foothills and higher ground of the Drakensberg mountains in the Eastern Cape and Lesotho.

The common name of *Aloe striata*, "Coral Aloe," is quite apt as the leaves are a pleasant sea green color and the leaf margins have a pink rim.

Aloiampelos tenuior is called the "Gardener's Aloe" as it will regularly flower out of season, if properly fed and watered.

Aloe striata

Plants are fairly low-growing, but in time will develop into short, shrubby specimens of which the stems remain clothed in the dried remains of dead leaves. The beautifully bluish- to sea green (turquoise) colored leaves are faintly striped, and have distinct light pinkish margins.

The many-branched inflorescences are usually flat-topped, and carry small, bright orange flowers in dense clusters in spring.

This is a species of South Africa's Eastern Cape and arid karroo regions. The flowers give color to the landscape at a time when few aloes are in flower, making it a desirable acquisition for any garden.

These plants do not have a seasonal preference for rainfall, and can tolerate downpours at any time of the year. It is a good plant for coastal gardens.

Aloiampelos tenuior

This scrambling climber has fairly long, weak stems, with leaves carried some distance apart. The thin, dagger-shaped leaves are deciduous in some forms.

The inflorescences are fairly short and thin, with the flowers sparsely dispersed, but the lack of dense inflorescences is made up for by the sheer number of inflorescences produced. The smallish flowers range in color from red through orange to yellow.

If there are no structures onto which the stems can grow, they will form large bushes that flower at any time of the year. In areas of climatic extremes, the plants die back to ground level during winter, reemerging in spring with fresh vigor.

Gasteria acinacifolia flowers are quite large and have only slight basal swellings.

The mottled leaves of *Gasteria bicolor* var. *bicolor* are the perfect camouflage to foil browsers.

Gasteria acinacifolia

Plants grow as very large, mostly single, rosettes. The leaves are very broad, with an oblique keel that stretches toward their tips, to give the leaves a typically triangular outline in cross-section.

The large flowers hang from horizontal inflorescence branches. They are bright orange, tinged with yellow.

The species is indigenous to South Africa's Eastern Cape coast. In its natural habitat it is most commonly encountered in low-growing dune scrub that is as high as the tops of the large rosettes. The climate where it occurs naturally is quite mild, and the species is unable to tolerate very low temperatures.

Propagation is by means of seed that germinates easily, or by removing and rooting some of the basal suckers.

In nature, the plants are often subjected to moisture laden sea wind and so they benefit from regular spraying when they are cultivated.

Gasteria bicolor var. bicolor

Plants usually grow as small to medium-sized, solitary rosettes that only rarely, very slowly, sucker from the base to form multiheaded specimens. The rosettes are almost invariably twisted into a spiral.

The leaves are usually quite long, dark green and densely mottled with light green to whitish spots.

The small pinkish flowers are basally swollen and carried in large open inflorescences.

This native of South Africa's southeast coast has beautifully colored leaves that give it an immense ability to blend in with its surroundings.

This is a useful survival strategy, as gasterias lack the bitter substance present in the leaves of other aloes that deter browsers.

It prefers dappled shade and will grow perfectly well under trees with open canopies.

The species grows quite quickly and flowers regularly once it has reached flowering maturity.

It can be propagated by removing and rooting the basal suckers, but it is also easy to propagate from seed.

Gonialoe varigata, the Partridge-Breasted Aloe, has been common in European greenhouses for several centuries.

In its natural habitat, *Haworthiopsis attenuata* forms large mats consisting of several small rosettes.

Gonialoe variegata

Plants are small, low-growing solitary specimens, but will readily form fairly large, multiheaded clumps. The leaves are reminiscent of species of *Gasteria*, being a fairly dark, blackish green, with irregular white spots. They are triangular in cross-section and compacted into three rows. The leaf margins carry a continuous white strip (as one finds in many gasterias).

The inflorescences carry the flowers in lax racemes. The dull pink to red flowers are somewhat curved.

Gonialoe variegata originates from South Africa's arid Karoo, where it grows under bushes that shield it from the intense sunlight. The plants can withstand extreme temperatures, but can easily be killed with too much water.

This is a widely cultivated species, with many European collections boasting a "Partridge-Breasted Aloe."

Haworthiopsis attenuata

Plants are strongly clustering and form large mats of low-growing rosettes that consist of tightly packed miniature dagger-shaped leaves. The leaves are deep green and crossbanded on both surfaces with prominent white ridge-like striations.

The inflorescences usually exceed the rosettes by several inches and often fail to support the flowers, which are a dull grayish white and distinctly two-lipped.

Plants do well in containers or as a ground cover in open beds. It is one of the most common *Haworthiopsis* species in the horticultural trade and a good one with which to gain confidence to start a succulent collection, as it is easy to grow and rapidly offsets, giving rise to large clumps.

Like many species from South Africa's Eastern Cape region, it has a year-round growing cycle.

Haworthiopsis fasciata can be distinguished from *Haworthiopsis attenuata* by its smooth upper leaf surfaces.

Haworthiopsis glabrata truly looks like a small species of aloe, with its rosettes and thickened leaves.

Haworthiopsis fasciata

Plants are solitary and only rarely branch to form specimens with two or three heads. The light, dull green leaves are tightly packed along a short stem, to which they remain attached, even when dry. The upper leaf surfaces are completely smooth, while the lower surfaces are crossbanded with thin, white ridges. The flowers are an insignificant grayish white color.

This species originates from the Eastern Cape of South Africa where it grows with a multitude of other succulent species. It tends to favor a slightly acidic soil mixture.

The name *Haworthiopsis fasciata* has often been misapplied to the more common *Haworthiopsis attenuata*. However, the two species are easy to separate on leaf characters alone, as *Haworthiopsis fasciata* leaves have smooth upper surfaces and are more deltoid in shape.

Haworthiopsis glabrata

Plants grow as small, strongly clumping rosettes. The leaves are thickened and a light green color. Both the upper and lower surfaces of the leaves are covered with small whitish to uniformly green protuberances. The flowers are a dull whitish green color.

This species originates from the Eastern Cape of South Africa.

Along with *Haworthiopsis attenuata*, this is arguably the best species of the genus for the budding succulent enthusiast to start with, as it is remarkably non-fussy as far as soil type, watering regime and temperature extremes are concerned.

Exposure to the full force of the elements can turn *Haworthiopsis viscosa* leaves an intense golden yellow.

ABOUT ALOES

The vast majority of species of *Aloe* occur in the summer rainfall regions of Africa. These species mainly flower during the dry winter months. This enables the plants to disperse their almost invariably small, black, wingless seeds during the ensuing months, just in time for the summer rains to facilitate seed germination and the establishment of the small seedlings with their initially very weak root systems. The opposite is of course true for some of the winter rainfall aloes, such as the spring-to-summer-flowering South African Tree-fan Aloe, *Kumara plicatilis*, which is restricted to the unique fynbos vegetation.

The horticultural benefit of the winter flowering of most *Aloe* species is that they provide magnificent splashes of color in domestic gardens during the drab winter months when little else is in flower, although they do need protection from frost.

MORE ABOUT ALOES . . .

Aloes come in all shapes and sizes. Their growth forms range from miniature rosette plants to massive trees of over 65 ft. (20 m) tall, and everything in between. The succulent creepers, *Aloiampelos tenuior* and *Aloiampelos ciliaris*, are scramblers that will form large mounds of tangled, leafy stems dotted with bright yellow or red flowers in sparse to dense clusters. These two species, and some others, such as *Aloiampelos striatula*, are the lazy succulent gardener's stalwarts, as they require little care, but just keep on flowering year after year without fail.

Haworthiopsis viscosa

Plants are immensely proliferous from the base and will form very large clumps of tightly packed stems. The leaves are very short, slightly to distinctly recurved and a bright yellow color if exposed to full sun.

The flowers are grayish white and distinctly two-lipped.

This species, from the arid, south-central parts of South Africa's Little Karoo, has a striking golden yellow leaf color if grown in hard conditions.

The elongated rosettes of *Haworthiopsis viscosa* can be easily removed and grown on to give rise to new plants. This is, in fact, the preferred method of propagation, even though the small, black seeds germinate easily.

CACTI AND SUCCULENTS HANDBOOK

In its natural habitat, *Tulista pumila* receives winter rain. In summer, the soil is often dry for long periods, making for very desiccated-looking plants.

Tulista pumila

Plants usually grow as small, but large for *Tulista*, solitary rosettes. The leaves are usually strongly incurved, sometimes making the rosettes appear ball-shaped. They vary considerably in color, from light green to reddish brown; the latter color coming out in strong sunlight.

The inflorescence is much-branched and carries numerous, small, grayish white flowers.

Many forms and horticultural selections make this species a desirable acquisition for any collection. Their charm comes mainly from the variously shaped, dirty white to bright white tubercles carried on the leaves.

A number of well-entrenched names have been applied to this species, which is indigenous to the Worcester area of South Africa's Western Cape, including *Haworthia margaritifera* and *Haworthia pumila*. Now known as *Tulista pumila*, it is one of the smaller of the *Aloe* relatives; *pumila* means small.

Kleinia stapeliifomis

ASTERACEAE

The Asteraceae, the largest family of flowering plants, has a near-universal geographical distribution range. To many aspiring collectors, the daisy family is not immediately associated with a succulent life form, but a surprisingly large number of species of this family are indeed stem and/or leaf succulents.

Members of the family occur in large numbers on most continents, where their head-shaped inflorescences often contribute to mass outdoor floral displays, one of the best-known examples being the mass spring flowering of daisies in South Africa's Namaqualand, an arid inland region which has a distinct winter rainfall regime.

Many species of Asteraceae occur in temperate areas that are not subjected to severe climatic extremes. In colder climates, it is advisable to keep most of them in a greenhouse where the plants can benefit from some form of heating during winter.

The most desirable succulent species of Asteraceae to grow are included in two genera, *Senecio* and *Kleinia*. The differences between the two genera are not always obvious, as they are mostly based on cryptic differences in the structure of the reproductive structures.

Many daisies are important in the horticultural trade, including South Africa's *Gerbera* species (Barberton daisies), and cultivars derived from them. Other daisy species, such as *Helianthus annuus* (the sunflower) and *Lactuca sativa* (lettuce) are important agricultural crops.

The beautiful bright yellow flowers of *Chrysanthemoides monolifera* contrast sharply with the green, woolly leaves.

The inflorescences of *Caputia medley-woodii* carry bright yellow, recurved ray florets.

Chrysanthemoides monolifera

Plants grow as large, robust shrubs or small trees, consisting of numerous soft-wooded branches that form a dense canopy. The slightly succulent leaves vary in color and outline, from bright green to rather dull green, and from nearly smooth-edged to deeply indented. A layer of dense woolly hairs covers the leaves of some forms of the species.

The inflorescences are typically head-shaped and carry prominent, straight, bright yellow ray florets.

This is a really fast grower that will quickly grow into a prized specimen in a succulent garden, but care should be taken in some parts of the world, particularly some regions of Australia, where it has become invasive.

Chrysanthemoides monolifera is easy to propagate from seed, which is the preferred method. Stem cuttings will also strike root, but should be dunked into commercially available root hormone powder, and the rooting medium must be kept moist. These precautions are usually required if the leaves on cuttings are only slightly succulent.

Caputia medley-woodii

The plants grow as robust shrubs that will either create a medium-sized, eye-catching feature on their own, or will scramble high into neighboring plants or shrubs. The leaves, which are fairly thick and whitish in color, are strikingly woolly and loosely arranged along the somewhat purplish stems.

The tiny flowers are arranged in head-shaped inflorescences, of which the ray florets have long, fused, recurved, butter yellow petals.

The species is indigenous to some of the densely woody areas along South Africa's eastern seaboard. It is a handsome plant that grows easily from stem cuttings.

Surprisingly, it can withstand low temperatures, making it suitable for planting in colder areas.

The head-shaped inflorescences of *Kleinia fulgens* are bright red, which contrasts sharply with the dull grayish green color of the leaves.

The leaves of *Kleinia fulgens* are indented, forming prominent, harmless, marginal teeth. The young inflorescences become erect only once the disk florets open.

The stems of the succulent daisy, *Kleinia stapeliifomis*, closely resemble those of any number of carrion flower species, members of the Apocynaceae.

Kleinia fulgens

Plants are low-growing and somewhat shrubby. The stems are thickened and fairly smooth, as the leaves—that are soon shed after they dry out—do not leave prominent leaf scars. The leaves are dull green, thickened, and their margins are jagged-edged.

The head-shaped inflorescences are carried in late winter and in spring. The small florets are a bright crimson red. The seeds are adorned with a little umbrella of white hairs, known as the pappus, which assist with seed dispersal.

The species, which is indigenous to South Africa's savanna or bushveld regions, is an excellent ground cover to use where a bright sunny spot requires the benefit of a plant with interesting leaves and stems. Plants grow easily from cuttings that can be placed directly in the soil where the plants are intended to grow.

Kleinia stapeliiformis

The stems of the plants are a deep brownish green, distinctly angled, and adorned with vertical rows of non-pungent protuberances.

Plants are leafless, but when they flower, there is no doubt that they belong to the daisy family. The bright red head-shaped inflorescences are borne on long stalks and attract attention from afar, even though ray florets are absent.

The species is indigenous to South Africa's savannas, where the prevalent climate is fairly mild. It makes a useful ground cover as, over time, it will proliferate by means of underground runners. Like all the *Senecio* species, it requires a frost-free environment if it is to survive cold northern winters.

The specific epithet of the species name is very apt: when not in flower, the plants look uncannily like species of the carrion flower family.

At first sight, *Senecio barbertonicus* looks like a pencil-bush euphorbia, but when in flower, the inflorescences clearly belong to the Asteraceae family.

The pencil-shaped, blue-green leaves of *Senecio crassulaefolius* compensate for the dull-colored inflorescences.

Senecio barbertonicus

Plants grow as typical, bushy shrubs that can reach the dimensions of small trees. The crowns are much-branched and quite dense. The leaves are a light green color and finger-shaped.

The head-shaped inflorescences are slender and borne erectly. They consist of tightly packed, bright yellow disk florets that lack conspicuous ray florets, but are nevertheless eye-catching.

Senecio barbertonicus, an inhabitant of the savanna or bushveld areas of southern Africa, is easy to cultivate in mild and subtropical regions, but cannot tolerate subzero temperatures.

Propagation is by means of stem cuttings that root rapidly in a friable, well-drained soil mixture.

Senecio crassulaefolius

Plants grow as erect or sprawling shrubs with thin stems that readily topple over, especially if they are grown under low light intensity.

The thin blue leaves radiate outward from the stems. Small, creamy white flowers are carried in tightly packed, head-shaped inflorescences.

The beauty of this species lies in the color of its leaves. Large beds of *Senecio crassulaefolius* (also known as *Senecio talinoides*), give a sense of calm movement, especially if planted on a gentle slope. It grows easily from stem cuttings, and can be planted directly in the ground.

This drought-tolerant species is indigenous to South Africa's western coastal regions, and arid interior.

The beauty of *Senecio haworthii* is undoubtedly in the color of the leaves, which will perfectly complement a trendy, modern white garden.

Senecio rowleyanus, known as a hanging basket plant, here grows as a shy miniature creeper in the protective branches of a Karoo shrublet.

Senecio haworthii

Plants grow as small to medium-sized shrubs. The stems are slightly rough to the touch and gray in color. The upper parts of the stems and branches carry finger-shaped dull gray to pure white leaves that easily drop if the plant is not handled with care.

The inflorescences are fairly small and a dull whitish yellow.

It is worth giving this species a place in any dry succulent or cactus garden. It is a South African native that grows very easily from stem cuttings that can be placed directly in the intended spot in a garden. As it is very drought-tolerant, it will thrive with little or no aftercare.

Plants must be given strong sunlight to bring out the best in their white leaf color. Also, if they grow in the shade, the stems of the plants tend to topple over. It has been suggested that *Senecio haworthii* should be included in the genus *Caputia*, but for the time being it is here retained in *Senecio*.

Senecio rowleyanus

In nature, plants grow as small clusters of thin, wiry stems that carry globular, teardrop-sized leaves some distance apart. The bright green leaves each have a single, small, laterally positioned, translucent window. (A beautifully variegated version has leaves with large white sections.)

The head-shaped inflorescences consist of numerous small disk florets that are an insignificant creamy white.

In its natural habitat plants often grow as shade-loving, low scramblers in karroid bushes in South Africa's arid interior. When so encountered, it is indeed difficult to imagine it as a useful hanging basket plant!

The common name of this species is very appropriately "String of Pearls," alluding to the shape of the leaves.

It grows easily and is one of the best succulents for hanging basket cultivation as the stems will rapidly and densely dangle over the edge of a container. It has been suggested that this species is merely a form of *Senecio radicans*, and that it should be included in the genus *Curio*.

The flowers of *Senecio rowleyanus*, showing its small, muted white, head-shaped inflorescences.

The bright yellow inflorescences of *Senecio tamoides* are carried in dense, ball-shaped clusters.

Senecio tamoides

Plants grow as large, multistemmed creepers that will rapidly cover a supporting structure, such as a trellis. The young stem and branches are soft and green, while the older ones have a thin, brownish bark. The leaves, which are shaped like those of common ivy, are bright green and shiny, and always appear to have been freshly polished.

The head-shaped inflorescences are carried in dense, tennis ball-sized clusters. They are sparkling yellow and have conspicuous ray florets.

The species is indigenous to the eastern seaboard of subtropical southern Africa, but has become naturalized in several mild climate regions around the world. It is particularly abundant along the Mediterranean coast.

Commonly known as the Canary Creeper, this is one of the best succulent-leaved creepers to plant in any garden.

Established plants take kindly to hedge trimming and will grow more densely if cut back occasionally.

Although it can survive on very little water, it cannot tolerate subzero temperatures.

Sempervivum tectorum

CRASSULACEAE

The Crassulaceae is a very large succulent plant family that occurs in both the Old and New Worlds. The species of this near-cosmopolitan family invariably have succulent leaves and, occasionally, succulent stems. Most species come from fairly mild climates, especially those that originate in Africa and Mexico. The indigenous European representatives, such as sedums and sempervivums, can easily be grown outdoors, even under northern climatic conditions. All other species need a frost-free environment if they are grown in colder climates.

The flower parts are separate and arranged in multiples of four or five. Although most species are small, low-growing plants with short stems, some attain the dimensions of small trees. Examples include the horticulturally very popular South African *Crassula ovata* and *Crassula arborescens*, and the Mexican *Sedum frutescens*.

In Africa and Madagascar the most handsome species are included in the genera *Crassula*, *Cotyledon*, and *Kalanchoe*. The Mexican and European species that are most often cultivated are included in the genera *Echeveria*, *Petrosedum*, *Sedum*, and *Sempervivum*.

With some notable exceptions, the representatives of the Crassulaceae that are popular in horticulture are grown for their interesting leaf and plant shapes rather than for their blooms. As indicated above, most *Sedum* and *Sempervivum* species are very hardy, while *Echeveria* will tolerate dry cold, such as found in a cold greenhouse.

The branches of *Cotyledon barbeyi* remain erect and carry clusters of tubular red flowers that hang down.

Cotyledon orbiculata, growing here alongside blue-leaved *Senecio crassulaefolius*, makes a useful, robust ground cover.

Cotyledon barbeyi

Plants grow as medium-sized shrubs. The stems are thin, smooth, and leafless lower down. Leaf shape and texture vary from smooth and pencil-shaped to hairy, broad, and shield-shaped.

The head-shaped inflorescences consist of a number of tubular red flowers with the petal tips flared open.

This species is indigenous to the southern African savanna. Like most *Cotyledon* species, it is remarkably cold hardy, although its natural distribution range has a fairly mild climate.

Cotyledon barbeyi can be confused with *Cotyledon orbiculata*. However, the flowers of *Cotyledon barbeyi* consistently have a prominent basal swelling.

Cotyledon orbiculata

Plants grow as medium-sized, branched, leafy shrubs. The stems, especially of forms with large leaves, are unable to support the upper leafy parts and tend to creep along the ground. The leaves vary in shape and size, from large, bright green and saucer-shaped to oval or pencil-shaped and bright white.

The tubular flowers are borne in small, head-shaped, downward-hanging clusters. They vary from yellow to red, with orange being most the common.

Widely distributed in the South African interior, the species grows easily from stem cuttings (the preferred way of propagation). It thrives in full sun, but can tolerate a fair amount of shade. The leaf shapes provide collectors with an array of different shapes and sizes.

The shrubby *Crassula arborescens* has blueish-green leaves and white flowers.

Crassula multicava makes a good succulent ground cover, especially in shady positions.

Crassula arborescens

Plants grow as medium-sized shrubs or small trees that typically have rounded, bushlike canopies. The leaves are blueish white to blue green and can attain the size of silver dollar coins. Tiny, scattered reddish pink spots occur on each leaf.

The star-shaped flowers, which are borne in small ball-shaped clusters, are white to creamy colored and, although they are very small, their clustered arrangement makes a spectacular show. They dry into persistent, rustic red balls on the plants.

This species is a worthwhile addition to any garden, given its interesting stems and leaves. A native of South Africa's arid Little Karoo, it has rightly attained worldwide popularity in succulent collections.

Even when planted as small cuttings, the preferred method of propagation, specimens quickly take on the dimensions of small, rounded shrubs.

Crassula multicava

Plants grow as dense tangles of soft, brittle branches and leaves. The dark, shiny green leaves are carried far apart on a light green stem and are quite large and rounded in outline.

The beautiful, fairylike flowers are small, star-shaped, and carried in loose clusters on tall stalks.

This species, another South African native, originates from the eastern seaboard, where it grows as part of the understory in thicket vegetation.

Although it comes from a very mild climate, it can tolerate surprisingly low temperatures. The plants thrive in deep shade. The leaves are large and rounded and will easily root where they drop. In fact, even small pieces of a leaf will produce new plants.

Crassula ovata, with its shiny foliage and pink flowers, is perfect for bonsai, as it grows well in small containers.

Kalanchoe beharensis leaves are a dull, gray-green color, with a felty, furry surface that is soft to the touch.

Crassula ovata

Plants grow as small trees or shrubs. With age, the decorative stems take on a rough appearance. The leaves are fairly small and rounded or egg-shaped (from which both the scientific name, and the common name, Money Plant, derive).

As with most *Crassula* species, the flowers are small, star-shaped, and a pinkish white color.

Indigenous to South Africa's Eastern Cape, *Crassula ovata* grows easily from stem cuttings or single leaves. It is a perfect companion to cacti and other succulents, and grows happily on a windowsill. It is one of the most widely grown, tolerant indoor plants in the northern hemisphere, as it grows happily in low levels of light intensity, but also thrives in direct sunlight.

Kalanchoe beharensis

Plants grow as medium-size to large-shrubby trees. The gray-brown trunks have sharp thornlike projections that develop from the scars left when the leaves are shed, and which become more prominent as the plants age.

Leaf outline is immensely variable, with a range of different forms, each with its characteristic shape, available in the horticultural trade. Take care when handling the plants, as the leaves are quite brittle. The flowers are borne on densely branched inflorescences.

This Madagascan plant is a perennial favorite in succulent gardens. It grows exceptionally well in mild, subtropical regions, and is drought tolerant, but in severe climates, subzero temperatures can damage the leaves and stems.

Plants will grow from stem cuttings, or from leaves that will easily strike root, particularly from the ends of the leaf stalks.

Kalanchoe longiflora leaves are an unusual sea green color, tinged with orange.

The yellow flowers of *Kalanchoe longiflora* are borne on elongated stalks. The flowers remain erect, unlike those of *Kalanchoe tubiflora*.

Kalanchoe longiflora

Plants are low-growing, soil-hugging, and multibranched. The stems are angled in cross-section and quite brittle. The leaves have shallow invaginations along their margins, giving them an interesting appearance.

However, the true beauty of the plant is in its leaf color, which is a striking turquoise blue, softly tinged with golden orange.

The bright yellow flowers, with flared-open tips, are carried on long stalks that can be trimmed off after the plants have flowered in autumn.

Kalanchoe longiflora is native to the eastern seaboard of South Africa. Although it prefers a milder climate, the species is remarkably hardy to cold and drought.

The species can easily be grown from stem cuttings that are established directly in beds.

One of the best uses of *Kalanchoe longiflora* in a garden is as a ground cover. As with many succulent species, the plants remain close to the ground in full sun, but can become etiolated in shady positions. It also grows quite happily in shade, but looks its best in full sun, which strongly brings out the orange tinge in the leaves.

The leaves of *Kalanchoe tubiflora* are beautifully colored with darker blotches on a light gray background.

The fleshy, off-white, egg-shaped leaves of *Pachyphytum oviferum* make it a coveted horticultural attraction.

Kalanchoe tubiflora

Plants grow as thin-stemmed shrubs that tend to topple over and sprawl on the ground. The light gray leaves are pencil-shaped and mottled with darker purplish brown blotches. Small, near-perfect plantlets are formed at the tips of the leaves.

The flowers are carried in small, head-shaped inflorescences at the tips of the stems. The dangling flowers are a beautiful bright red to orange color.

The plantlets that form at the tips of the leaves are easily shed, and rapidly produce a small forest of plants around the mother plant. This species therefore clearly has the ability to become an invasive garden plant and it should not be cultivated in open beds in mild and subtropical climates.

If this Madagascan plant did not produce so many offshoots, it would be a very desirable acquisition for any garden, as the interesting leaves and inflorescences contribute to its beauty.

Pachyphytum oviferum

Plants are low-growing and fat-leaved. The leaves easily become detached from the stem, exposing a short, whitish gray stem with small, but obvious leaf scars. The oval leaves are an interesting off-white color, and resemble small bird eggs.

The nodding inflorescence is quite short and carries a number of small, loosely arranged flowers. The flowers are fairly insignificant in size and color but, rather interestingly, are almost entirely enclosed by large, greenish white floral bracts.

These low-growing plants have very fat, egg-shaped leaves, undoubtedly a feature that makes them desirable to grow as part of a collection.

A leaf that becomes detached from a plant will quickly form roots and grow into a healthy new plant.

This Mexican species is exceptionally easy in cultivation. It grows well in open beds in mild climates, but should be protected from the excessive rainfall and low temperatures found in more severe climates.

Sedum praealtum subsp. *praealtum* usually grows as a small to medium-sized, densely-leaved shrub. It can also be trimmed into a neat, low hedge.

Sedum praealtum subsp. praealtum

Plants grow as small to medium-sized erect shrubs. The branches are fairly thin, but stiff and remain erect. The flattened, slightly spoon-shaped leaves are a light, bright green and always appear to have been freshly buffed.

The small yellow flowers are carried in inverted cone-shaped inflorescences.

This Mexican species, which must rate as one of the most commonly cultivated species of Crassulaceae, is horticulturally very versatile. It can be grown as a small, stand-alone shrub or, if planted close together, as a continuous hedge.

The plant has been introduced to many parts of the world as an ornamental plant and is very hardy, as far as both temperature and rainfall are concerned.

The inflorescences of *Sedum praealtum* subsp. *praealtum* are cone-shaped, and consist of a multitude of small yellow flowers.

DIDIERACEAE

In terms of genera, the family Didiereaceae is best represented on Madagascar, Ile de Rouge, or the Red Island, where four genera have been recorded. Recently, the genera *Portulacaria* and *Ceraria* were reclassified in the Didieriaceae, so that it now also has a representation in neighboring southern Africa. *Portulacaria* has succulent stems and leaves, but unlike the Madagascan representatives, species in this genus lack spines on their stems. *Portulacaria afra*, commonly known as Porkbush or Elephant's Food, grows as a large, shrubby specimen, but can also be kept in a small container for many decades. The stems are pliable and can be variously trained into a fascinating bonsai tree. It can easily be pruned and manipulated into interesting shapes in the garden, making it a useful architectural plant. In its natural habitat, it is an excellent fodder plant for game, including elephants, as its common name indicates. Species of the genus *Portulacaria* require protection from excessive amounts of rain. Even if they are kept dry in winter, frost is still sure to induce considerable leaf drop and the tips of the stems will die back.

A heavily grazed specimen of *Portulacaria afra* in valley bushveld vegetation in South Africa's Eastern Cape province.

Portulacaria afra leaves are densely arranged on the branches and provide the perfect green "canvas" against which a gardener can paint with other species that have contrasting foliage or color.

Inset photo. Close-up of the flowers of *Portulacaria afra*.

Portulacaria afra

Plants grow as robust, multibranched, erect shrubs or small trees. The stems are covered with a brownish bark that peels of from time to time, especially after cold spells. The leaves are small, bright green, and very much thickened.

Plants produce clusters of small purple flowers in midsummer.

The species is indigenous to the eastern seaboard of southern Africa.

Propagation is through stem cuttings or truncheons that root exceptionally easily. Plants do well in open beds and containers. They can even be planted in small trays and turned into bonsai.

A number of selected forms of Portulacaria afra are available in the trade, including forms with leaves that are partly yellow. These grow more slowly than their green counterparts and are perfect for cultivation in hanging baskets. However, the most striking form is arguably the one that sprawls along the ground and over rocks, never rising more than a few inches above the soil surface, making the perfect succulent ground cover.

DRACAENACEAE

Dracaena transvaalensis

This small family of mostly tropical African species is represented in succulent plant collections by species mainly from two genera: *Sansevieria* and *Dracaena*. Species of the former are mostly small, low-growing plants with sharp-tipped, spotted leaves, while the latter are small to large fat-trunked trees.

Like representatives of the Agavaceae, the century plant family, the leaves of many members of the Dracaenaceae are exceptionally fibrous. To this day, people in areas where, for example, *Sansevieria* species occur naturally, harvest the leaves and ingeniously extract and convert the fibers into very strong and durable lengths of rope.

A horticultural benefit of species of the Dracaenaceae is that many of them are very tolerant of shady positions. In their natural habitats they often grow as part of the lower layer of savanna and forest vegetation. This ability to grow well where there are comparatively low levels of light makes them perfectly suited for cultivation in the garden under shady trees.

Most *Dracaenaceae* species occur naturally in fairly mild, more or less frost-free areas. To cultivate them successfully requires protection against low temperatures, especially in areas that receive rain in winter. In areas that experience high summer humidity, they will flourish under glass, and many species do well when cultivated indoors.

Most species of *Dracaena* are only weakly succulent, the leaf-succulent *Dracaena transvaalensis* (see photo above) being an exception. The most prominent and widely cultivated succulent in the *Dracaenaceae* is the spectacular, thick-stemmed *Dracaena draco* (Dragon Tree) from the Canary Islands. The family Dracaenaceae is sometimes included in a more inclusive, but rather unwieldy family, the Asparagaceae, an approach not followed here.

A large canopy of stout branches is perched on top of an impressive, unbranched trunk of *Dracaena draco*.

The flowers of *Dracaena draco* are small, white, and carried in large, multibranched inflorescences.

Dracaena draco

When it comes to succulent trees, it is difficult to beat the bold, masculine growth form of the Dragon Tree, *Dracaena draco*, which grows several meters tall, with a canopy of often as many meters across.

The trunks are smooth and gray. A rosette of grayish-green leaves is carried at the end of each branch. The leaves are smooth, non-succulent, and pliable.

The inflorescence is multibranched and carries small, white flowers in dense clusters. The flowers make way for fleshy, orange, marble-sized fruits.

This is the well known Dragon Tree from the Canary Islands. In its general growth form it is a tree in the true sense of the word: it forms a single, thick bole that supports a large, dense crown of fairly thick branches, each of which carries a rosette of thin leaves.

Its succulence lies in its stems and, if grown well, is a real asset in any subtropical, coastal, or temperate garden.

Dragon Trees are easily propagated from seed. Newly established trees should be protected in areas that experience subzero temperatures.

In its natural habitat, *Dracaena aletriformis* grows as a component of forest understories.

Dracaena aletriformis

Plants grow mostly as single-stemmed treelike specimens. The trunks are smooth and erect, but not as thick as those of the Dragon Tree.

The leaves are long, quite broad, and strap-shaped with thin white margins. They are a beautiful dark green color and are gracefully recurved, drooping from the terminal rosettes at the ends of the stems.

The small creamy white flowers are carried in dense, branched inflorescences. They are succeeded by small, but decorative, orange to red berries.

This southern African semi-succulent species is the perfect shade-loving tree. With its smooth stems, up to 6 ½ ft. (2 m) tall, it makes a fine specimen in a succulent garden, preferably located under a taller tree.

This is one of the few species that looks better when the dried (dead) leaves are removed from the plants; with most other succulent species, such as aloes, removing dead leaves results in plants that are decidedly artificial looking.

Sansevieria hyacinthoides

Plants grow as erect, robust, grasslike tufts. The leaves are carried in rather compact rosettes that tend to multiply rapidly, giving rise to impenetrable thickets. Leaf color varies from light green to a nearly metallic blue. The leaves are mottled with lighter green or silvery crossbands that tend to become confluent to form zebra-like stripes, especially in the upper parts of the leaves.

The flowers are creamy white and fairly large, and are carried in a short to medium-length inflorescence.

This species is indigenous to the African savannas where it favors rocky outcrops.

It is commonly known as Rhinoceros Grass, and for good reason: with its erect, sturdy leaves reaching a length of nearly 20 in. (50 cm), only a large animal like a rhinoceros would venture into a dense stand.

In cultivation its unique growth form contrasts pleasantly with those of cacti and other succulents.

Sansevieria hyacinthoides is exceptionally hardy, being able to survive very dry spells with no apparent ill effects.

Sansevieria trifasciata

Plants grow as medium-sized, erect tufts of leathery, slightly succulent leaves. Small clumps are formed via the production of underground runners. The leaves are a dark green color, with white to silvery blotches, and the leaf margins are often variously colored yellow or creamy yellow.

Because of the ease with which the leaf coloration and size can become aberrant, a profusion of horticultural selections have been named in this species.

The flowers are fairly large, creamy white, and carried on a short stalk. Unfortunately the species is shy to flower in cultivation.

This Central African species must qualify as one of the most tolerant of all plants as far as horticultural abuse is concerned. It thrives on neglect but, if given proper treatment (i.e., sufficient light, food, and water), it is a stunning plant with its silvery white or yellow speckled or striped leaves.

Indeed, these plants are not grown so much for their flowers as for their highly decorative leaves, which make them popular as windowsill, indoor, or outdoor bedding plants.

Referring to their sharp-tipped, tongue-shaped leaves, the species has been given the common name "Mother-in-Law's Tongue."

Propagation is very easy through division of the underground runners.

Sansevieria trifasciata 'Laurentii' grows as well indoors as it does outside in open garden beds.

The leaves of the regular form of *Sansevieria trifasciata* are dark green, mottled with horizontal creamy white sections.

Euphorbia cooperi

EUPHORBIACEAE

At least in terms of the appearance of their expanded plant bodies, the succulent representatives of the spurge, or milkweed, family are the African equivalent of the cactus family. Like cacti, the stems of most *Euphorbia* species are leafless and the stems are often ribbed. However, *Euphorbia* can be easily separated from cacti in that they are laden with a corrosive milky latex and the flowers are actually small inflorescences, called cyathia. Cyathia (singular cyathium) are often yellowish in color; the highly colored "flowers" of the poinsettia (*Euphorbia pulcherrima*) are in fact not flowers at all, but rather leafy bracts that surround the cyathia. Further, the color of the pseudo-flowers of euphorbias are often imparted by the small, but prominent, variously shaped nectar glands that surround the male and female flowers in the cyathia. With over 2,000 species, the genus *Euphorbia* is one of the largest genera of flowering plants. Like cacti, *Euphorbia* plants are mostly also spiny, but their thorns have a different origin from the spines of cacti; for example, they do not arise from areoles.

Milkweeds are widely distributed and occur almost the world over, but the desirable succulent species are mostly confined to Africa and the island of Madagascar.

Some species have both male and female reproductive organs in their flowers, while others are either male or female, implying that at least two plants are required to produce seed.

If grown in colder climates, most *Euphorbia* species need a frost-free environment, preferably in a greenhouse, although those originating from East Africa and Magagascar need a reasonably high minimum temperature in order to thrive. With the exception of *Euphorbia myrsinites*, all the species of the family Euphorbiaceae discussed here occur in temperate regions where they are not exposed to severely cold, wet conditions for any length of time. Most species will survive winters in an unheated greenhouse but some, like *Euphorbia trigona* (not discussed), prefer temperatures of 41°F (5°C) or above.

The margins of *Euphorbia cooperi* branches are adorned with short spines, as well as cyathia (the inflorescences).

Euphorbia cooperi is drought-tolerant, but does not appreciate subzero temperatures for long periods.

Euphorbia ingens is typical of southern and eastern African savannas. The outline of the tree is eggcup shaped.

Euphorbia cooperi

These grow as trees of which the main stems are usually constricted at regular intervals, giving them the look of the legs of the Michelin man. A single trunk is formed that supports a crown of thick, angular branches that droop slightly before reaching for the sky. In silhouette, this gives the crown of the plant the shape of a massive upside-down heart.

Small, yellow cyathia (the inflorescences of euphorbias) are produced toward the tips of the branches.

A number of *Euphorbia* species attain large treelike dimensions. They can be cultivated from branch cuttings, but do ensure the wound is properly sealed before they are placed onto a moist, sandy mixture to root.

Euphorbia cooperi species can be grown from branches (like *Euphorbia ingens*), but it is also very easy to grow them from seed. Seedlings grow quickly into miniature treelike Euphorbias that can be kept in pots for many years, making them suitable for cultivation in smaller gardens.

Euphorbia ingens

Plants grow as massive trees consisting of a single stem that supports a large canopy of erect branches, which curve upward, giving the appearance of a large, overgrown eggcup. The angled, prominently ribbed branches are dull green, turning gray with age. The edges of the ribs carry vertical rows of small very pungent spines. The flowers are carried in small, yellow inflorescences.

The plants are easy to cultivate and can even be grown from branches. The cut surface of the branch must be left to dry properly before it is placed on a well-drained, friable soil mixture that contains adequate material, such as gritty sand, to promote good drainage.

Being quite frost sensitive, euphorbia plants must be given protection if the temperature falls below 32°F (0°C) in winter. The rib margins and growing tips of the stems are the first to be damaged by very low temperatures, and stems that have been damaged in this way almost invariably die.

Euphorbia meloformis, a low-growing milkweed, resembles a globular cactus.

The bright red flowers carried on the tangled mass of stems of *Euphorbia milii* var. *milii* will brighten up any garden.

Euphorbia meloformis

These globular cactus "look-alike" plants generally grow as low, ground-hugging domes in the shape of a bishop's cap (mitre). Older specimens tend to be more columnar in shape. The plant bodies are angled and usually a dusty, light green. The stems are crossbanded with light brown horizontal stripes.

The flowers, borne separately on male and female plants, are small and insignificant. When the fruits split open, the seeds are ejected with some force.

Euphorbia meloformis originates from the Eastern Cape of South Africa.

The plants are most often solitary and, to the uninitiated, look very much like small cacti.

Euphorbia milii var. milii

Plants grow as dense, multibranched shrubs. The branches are fairly thin and pliable and will quickly grow into a tangled mass. The entire lengths of the stems are armed with sharp thorns. The light green leaves are club-shaped in outline and non-succulent. They remain on the plants for longer than those of most euphorbias, but are eventually shed to leave the stems leafless, as would be expected of the succulent members of this genus.

The flowers vary from bright red through pale pink and orange to yellow.

This Madagascan species has two claims to fame: firstly it grows quickly and will rapidly cover a denuded area, and secondly, it flowers very readily.

And, when it flowers, it is a truly spectacular plant to have in a garden. Selected miniaturized forms have been bred and make exquisite subjects for growing as container plants.

It is easy to establish plants from cuttings that grow rapidly and will flower within the year. Plants are frost tender, so some protection should be given in areas where temperatures fall below zero in winter.

Dense clusters of yellow bracts are produced around the cyathia near the stem tips of *Euphorbia myrsinites*.

Euphorbia stellispina spines are arranged in a star-shaped fashion. The yellow cyathia are carried near the stem tips.

Euphorbia myrsinites

Plants are low-growing to creeping shrubs that could also form a useful ground cover. The stems are fairly thin and heavy with sharply tipped leaves. For this reason the stems are hardly able to remain erect. The leaves are a distinct blue-green color and only slightly succulent.

The floral bracts are bright yellow and produced in dense clusters near the stem tips.

A native of southern and eastern Europe, *Euphorbia myrsinites* is unfortunately not easy to grow from cuttings. It is very hardy and will easily survive cold winters.

The blueish leaves make this species a very useful addition to any garden. It can even be grown in a hanging basket, with the stems dangling over the edge of the suspended container.

Euphorbia stellispina

Plants grow as small to medium-sized shrublets, with columnar, ribbed plant bodies not unlike those of many species of cactus. The stems can reach a height of 20 in. (50 cm) and are adorned with spines that terminate in sharp, variously forked tips giving the spines a characteristic starlike appearance. The small cyathia are produced near the tips of the stems.

These delightful plants are native to the arid Great Karoo and adjacent karroid areas of South Africa.

These plants are not as easy in cultivation as one might hope, given their beauty. Care should be taken that they are not overwatered, and the soil mixture must be well drained. Plants can withstand very low temperatures; well below 32°F (0°C).

Sticks-of-Fire (*Euphorbia tirucalli*) stems have bright red tips, a feature that intensifies in times of drought or cold.

Euphorbia virosa plants have an apparently stemless, candelabra-shaped growth form.

Euphorbia tirucalli

Plants grow as medium-sized to very large trees. The trunks are smooth and dull green, turning gray as the plants age. The trees are completely leafless, but the green, pencil-shaped twigs have taken over the role of leaves.

Plants are either male or female and produce small, insignificant inflorescences in spring.

This is another spectacular African succulent tree. Its main benefit is that it is leafless and, apart from dropping a few dried branchlets, produces no litter.

Truncheons planted directly into the ground, where a tree is required, will quickly take root, producing a dense crown of pencil-shaped branches.

A beautiful selected form, "Sticks-of-Fire," has branchlets that turn bright red when kept fairly dry, or when exposed to bright sunlight.

Euphorbia virosa

Plants grow as medium-sized to very large, multistemmed shrubs. The stems are angled and carry vertical rows of short, very pungent thorns. In addition, these innocent-looking plants contain very virulent milky latex.

The stems are a pleasant green color, even under conditions of drought stress. The cyathia are also produced along the margins of the stem ribs.

Euphorbia virosa is indigenous to the arid western coastal parts of southern Africa, through Namibia, as far north as Angola. This species of *Euphorbia* is exceptionally well adapted to dry conditions and can get by on very little water.

Stem cuttings do not root easily, but the species is easy to grow from seed.

Euphorbia woodii belongs to the group of finger-euphorbias, so called because the short branches radiate outward.

Jatropha podagrica flowers are brilliant red, which contrasts sharply with the large, deeply lobed, bright green leaves.

Euphorbia woodii

Plants are low-growing, bright green shrublets, with a strong, central stem portion that merges with the underground, rootlike part. The finger-like branches radiate from the stem. The central growth point of the stem has surface protuberances and is rough to the touch.

The tiny flowers, borne in small inflorescences, are bright yellow.

This species grows easily in mild and subtropical regions, unlike many of its relatives. A native of the eastern seaboard of South Africa, it is usually propagated from seed.

Most finger-euphorbias occur naturally in rather arid areas; *Euphorbia woodii* being a notable exception.

Jatropha podagrica

Plants grow as small to medium-sized bottle-trunked specimens. In young plants, the stems are often covered with a light gray to brownish, peeling bark, while the stems of older plants tend to be smooth. Even as young plants the stems mostly have a pronounced basal swelling, becoming thinner upward.

The bright green leaves have deep marginal invaginations and are quite large for such a small plant.

The flower petals are a deep scarlet red which, along with the stem architecture, have made these plants very popular in cultivation.

This species hails from tropical Central America and does well in cultivation in similar climates. Plants are very easy to grow from seed and will become established as garden escapees where the climate is conducive for them to flourish.

Jatropha podagrica cannot tolerate low temperatures at all: a good specimen can be turned to a soft, rotting mass by just one night of frost.

Pedilanthus tithymaloides subsp. *smallii* here clearly shows the zigzag shape of the branches.

Pedilanthus tithymaloides subsp. tithymaloides

Plants grow as small, more or less erect shrubs consisting of thin, green branches with grayish-white blotches. The branches tend to branch in a zigzag fashion. The leaves are slightly fleshy and tend to be persistent in tropical and subtropical areas. In more severe climates the leaves are shed when the plants are in flower.

The flowers are small, bright red, and shaped like very small inverted cones.

New plants can easily be established from soft or hard wood cuttings that should be placed in a well drained soil mixture which is kept damp. Given its preference for more tropical climates, it cannot tolerate cold, wet conditions, and easily succumbs to rot.

This is a good member of the milkweed family to grow in mild climates, as it is a native of Mexico and the northern parts of South America with such a climate. Plants grow quickly and can be trimmed into a nice hedge.

NOLINACEAE

Dasylirion wheeleri

The Nolinaceae is a fairly small family of only about 50 species included in four genera that were traditionally included in the *Agavaceae*.

The Nolinaceae is also sometimes treated as a subfamily, the Nolinoideae, of the family Asparagaceae. It is here retained as a family in own right.

Horticulturally, the species of *Nolinaceae* are excellent specimen plants that will do any garden proud. These are some of the hardiest succulents available in the horticultural trade, being able to tolerate very low temperatures, provided they are kept dry in winter. In cold, wet areas, they should be protected from excessive rain.

Harvested stems of mature plants of *Dasylirion wheeleri*, commonly known as the Desert Spoon, is the raw material used in the production of the distilled alcoholic beverage known as sotol. This species grows in northern Mexico and the southern USA. The method of production of sotol approximates that of mezcal, which is produced from distilled agave "hearts." Commercially, the best known type of mezcal is tequila. A Desert Spoon plant can take well over 10 years to be regarded as mature. In contrast to the monocarpic species of *Agave* that flowers only once in its lifetime, Desert Spoons produce a flower stalk every few years.

Two of the more commonly cultivated Nolinaceae species are discussed here.

Old specimens of *Beaucarnea recurvata* branch high up from a bulbous, bottle-like trunk that is topped with clusters of leaves.

Beaucarnea recurvata

Plants grow as medium to very large, bottle-trunked specimens that are topped with clusters of light green leaves, which sprout from the top of a stem and then gracefully curve downward, obscuring part of the stems. The leaves are thin, flat, and pliable.

The flowers are produced in large inflorescences. However, they are quite small and fairly insignificant.

This Mexican species is grown for the strong lines of its trunk, not its flowers. In older specimens, the lower part of the stem takes on a corky appearance, but even young plants, with their globular stems supporting a thinner vertical extension, are worthwhile additions to a garden or patio.

They are cold hardy and drought tolerant, but may need protection from the coldest northern winters.

The common name of *Beaucarnea recurvata*, Ponytail Palm, is very apt, as the plants carry ponytail-like clusters of leaves at the tips of the stems.

Numerous rosettes will form from the swollen trunk if the central growing tip is damaged.

Dasylirion wheeleri has narrow, ribbonlike leaves that radiate from the trunk to form a sphere-like specimen. The leaves are very sharply toothed along their margins.

Dasylirion wheeleri

Plants grow as very large, ball-shaped, rosulate leaf clusters. The leaves are thin, flattened, only slightly succulent, and a distinctive blue color. The leaf margins are covered with sharp spines that curve toward the tips of the leaves which, in turn, carry small feather duster-like clusters of loose fibers.

After many years (up to eight) of cultivation, a single, tall inflorescence is produced. The flowers are very small, quite insignificant, and densely clustered around the flowering pole.

As a result of the characteristic curvature of the marginal leaf spines, it is difficult to put your hand into a rosette but, thankfully, very easy to take it out again! The spines break off readily and can become firmly lodged in one's flesh.

This species is exceptionally cold and drought hardy. It occurs naturally in the southern USA and Mexico, where an alcoholic beverage, "sotol," is distilled from the fermented soft inner tissue of a stem.

Peperomia retusa

PIPERACEAE

One thing is certain: the succulent representatives of the Piperaceae (peppers and peperomias) are not grown for their big, brightly colored flowers, which are minute, and arranged in short, toothpick-like inflorescences. Instead, their fascination is much more centered on their interesting leaf morphologies. Most species of Piperaceae originate from tropical or subtropical areas, making them suitable for cultivation indoors or in heated greenhouses.

Peperomia are rock-loving and grow with their roots clinging to near-vertical rock faces where precipitation drains away rapidly. Alternatively, plants will take root in the small pockets of soil and decaying leaf litter that accumulate in rock cracks. Most peperomias are shade-loving, and often grow in dry sites in forests. Given their preference for shady locations, peperomias are often sold in nurseries as indoor plants.

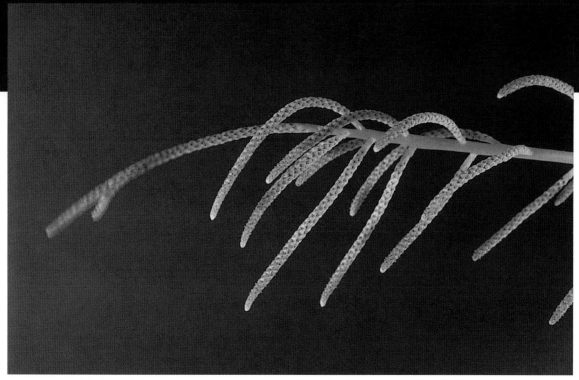

A *Peperomia dolabriforme* inflorescence carrying tiny flowers. This species is not grown for its colorful flowers.

Peperomia dolabriforme

In cultivation, plants are small, low growing, and soil hugging, but in their natural habitat they can reach a height of 20 in. (50 cm). The species originates in northern Peru.

The stems are very short and brittle, and the light green leaves are the shape of a pizza folded in half. Along the rounded margin, the leaves have a prominent, translucent window.

The flowers are minute, and only visible as little black dots arranged on a toothpick-like inflorescence.

Plants grow quite easily, but do best in dappled shady positions. They prefer ample water and a well-drained soil mixture rich in organic matter.

The leaves of *Peperomia dolabriforme*, commonly known as the Prayer Peperomia, have an interesting folded appearance.

Portulaca Pizazz™ 'Red Flare' is a horticultural selection of the South American *Portulaca umbraticola*.

PORTULACACEAE

The Portulacaceae, the Purslane family, used to be a very diverse group, but its classification was recently refined. As one example of this refinement, the well-known African Pork Bush species (in the genus *Portulacaria*) are now grouped in the family Didieriaceae. The redefined Portulacaceae now includes only one genus, *Portulaca*. By far the best-known succulent that is included in the Portulacaceae is *Portulaca oleracea*, commonly known as Purslane. This is a troublesome weed in many parts of the world and, with its succulent leaves and stems, quite hardy. In addition, parts of the stem will root where they are dropped and in established plants the strong taproot is difficult to dislodge once plants have matured. The leaves and young shoots are edible, though, and often boiled as a vegetable or eaten fresh in a salad. It is therefore a very useful succulent, but since it can easily escape from cultivation through copious seed production, it is best planted in pots rather than in garden beds. *Portulaca oleracea*, and several other portulacaceous species, have succulent, coin-shaped leaves. In other species, the leaves are very much reduced, while some have distinctly succulent stems or roots. The various very showy cultivars of *Portulaca grandiflora* are generally annuals and avoid the unfavorable winter season as dormant seed. They are very popular bedding plants in domestic and public gardens where they provide fantastic floral displays.

Portulaca grandiflora flowers come in a range of colors that will brighten up any garden in summer.

Portulaca grandiflora

Plants are low-growing, soil-hugging leaf succulents. The stems are very short, soft, and brittle. The small leaves are cylindrical and a bright green color.

The flowers are borne singly and are quite large, up to 1½ in. (4 cm) across, for such small plants. Color ranges from deep pink to bright purple. Some selections have double flowers while others have multicolored flowers.

The South American *Portulaca grandiflora* is predominantly annual and has to be sowed every year to ensure a crop of color in a garden. Seed, which is sold in packets in garden shops, germinates easily. A vast range of flower colors has been selected from the pure species with its purplish pink flowers.

It is difficult to beat the wonderful floral display that can be obtained from a dense planting of portulacas. Plants require little aftercare and will happily grow in full sun, and flower where the seed germinates.

The small, succulent leaves of *Portulaca oleracea* are edible.

Portulaca oleracea

Known as the Common Purslane, this very variable species usually remains flat growing to soil hugging, but will sometimes develop into slightly erect shrublets. Plants are annual herbs with reddish, spreading stems. The fresh or cooked young shoots and succulent leaves are edible and nutritious. Today it is a weed established in most parts of the subtropics and tropic regions of the world. It was likely introduced to the rest of world from Europe, as it was widely grown by early seafarers as a source of vitamin C. The alternating leaves carried along the stems are more or less coin shaped, but narrow toward the base. The yellow flowers are quite small and not long-lasting. Fruit is a capsule that opens to release the small, black seeds.

CACTI AND SUCCULENTS HANDBOOK

The bright yellow flowers of *Portulacaria oleracea* are quite small.

Portulacaria oleracea is very hardy and will grow in any soil, even pure sand.

COMPANION SUCCULENTS

The small black aphids on these inflorescences of *Gonialoe variegata* can be easily treated with a systemic or contact insecticide. Similar sapsuckers attack most cacti and succulent species.

COMMON PESTS AND DISEASES

The good news is that well-grown cacti and succulents are extremely hardy and do not easily succumb to pests and diseases. The first step toward having a healthy collection is to ensure that the plants are not unduly subjected to environmental stress, as a strong plant is more likely to withstand the onslaught of insect or fungal attacks than one suffering from extreme desiccation, for example. Put simply, prevention is better than cure.

However, make no mistake, cacti and succulents can be attacked by a number of pests and diseases. Some of these are specific to certain families, genera, or species, while others are generalists that do not discriminate when it comes to obtaining their sustenance.

Pest infestations often occur where they are difficult to detect, such as on the underside of leaves, or where the leaves attach to the stems. Some of the more problematic and non-discriminating pests are mentioned here.

Scale insects

These are generally small round or oblong insects that cling tightly to the leaf or stem surfaces. They are most commonly white, brown, or reddish in color and their bodies are generally covered by a tough, protective shield. This means that insecticides applied to kill them require a wetting agent, to make the poison "stick" to the insects. (Try dishwashing liquid if you need to add a wetting agent.)

Scale insects have an immense ability to multiply, and a small patch of scale bugs on a plant one day might cover an entire leaf or stem a week later, so treat these bugs as soon as possible.

Although a strong jet of water will dislodge most scale insects from a plant, an outbreak can be most efficiently treated by applying a systemic insecticide. This should halt the spread of scale insects.

Mealybugs

Mealybugs can damage the above- and below-ground parts of a plant. The most destructive ones seem to be the below-ground bugs that feed off roots. The reason is probably that they tend to go undetected for a long time.

A sure sign that the root balls of plants need to be inspected for mealybugs is when plants begin to look lethargic and do not respond to irrigation and fertilizer.

Mealybugs are more of a problem in containers and in greenhouses; plants growing in open garden beds seem much better able to cope with these destructive and unobtrusive insects in their woolly coats.

This pest can be treated with a systemic insecticide or, if you have a steady hand, the insects visible on aboveground plant parts can be dabbed with methylated spirits (denatured alcohol).

Aphids

Aphids are small insects that feed on the sap of a plant, piercing the stem, leaf, or inflorescence surfaces and bleeding them dry. Ants are attracted to the sugary substance that many aphid species exude once attached to a plant, which further disperses the aphids.

Fortunately, aphids are mostly soft-bodied, and can easily be destroyed by treating plants with any one of a range of commercially available contact or systemic insecticides.

Snout weevils

Snout weevils or snout beetles (the terms are used interchangeably) typically attack the larger aloes and agaves, especially those growing in the open. Mature beetles burrow into the crown of a rosette where they lay their eggs. The "worms" that eventually hatch burrow into the center of the leaf crowns and feed on the young, soft new growth of these otherwise very hardy plants.

Once the pests are detected, it is generally too late to save the plant as the crowns collapse into a smelly heap ready for the trash can—note, not the compost heap!

One of the few ways of treating infected plants is to inject neat systemic insecticide with a syringe

If left unchecked, white scale insects can rapidly spread to cover an entire plant. This specimen of *Aloe littoralis* has been obliterated by this unwelcome pest.

An attack by the Agave weevil is often only detected once a perfectly healthy-looking plant has been all but destroyed. The borer burrows into the core of a tightly-packed rosette, making it difficult to see the damage. In this instance a specimen of *Agave salmiana* was completely destroyed.

into a tiny hole drilled into the stem of a plant.

As a preventative measure plants can also be dusted at regular intervals with any commercially available wettable powder insecticide.

Nematodes

These small, worm-like creatures typically attack the roots of plants, rapidly infesting them and resulting in globular outgrowths resembling nitrogen-fixing nodules. This excessive organismal activity impairs the ability of a plant to obtain sufficient nutrients from the soil to maintain healthy growth.

One of the early symptoms of nematodes is a plant that looks decidedly lethargic, or is simply "refusing" to grow.

Infected plants must be lifted and the infected roots severed and destroyed. Leave the plants in a shady location to allow the wounds to callus over before replanting them.

Unfortunately, it is not easy to get rid of nematodes in open beds. One solution is to grow

CACTI AND SUCCULENTS HANDBOOK

CACTI AS INVASIVE ALIENS

Many cacti have become naturalized in various parts of the world. This has happened particularly in areas that have similar climates, or more temperate climates (for example, subtropical), than the plants experience in their native habitats. In addition, the cacti's natural predators are usually absent from these new habitats, which means the cacti can rapidly proliferate and multiply, often at the expense of the area's native flora.

A step beyond being simply naturalized is that they can rapidly become troublesome weeds. Because cacti carry protective armature, it is often not that easy to physically eradicate them once they have gone wild in their adopted countries.

One means of countering invasive cacti is via biological control (which introduces species-specific predators originating from the plants' natural habitats). This method has brought success in taming one noxious cactus, the prickly pear (*Opuntia ficus-indica*, above) in both South Africa and Australia, but it is very expensive to implement.

highly aromatic species, such as *Tulbaghia violacea* (wild garlic), *Tagetes patula* (daisy bush), or *Plectranthus neochilus* (spur flower) in the same beds. These mostly herbaceous species are remarkably hardy and very decorative annuals or perennials that are sure to enhance the displays in your cactus and succulent garden.

Fungal infections

Under dry atmospheric conditions, fungal attacks are not a big problem, but they become more evident during wet, inclement weather. Fungal infections usually show themselves as small or large, round, dark reddish, brown, or black rings on the leaves or stems. Treat these spots with a fungicide as soon as they become visible, as fungal infections are difficult to get rid of once they are firmly established.

A fungal attack on *Aloe marlothii*. This malady should be treated with a fungicide as soon as it is detected.

INDEX

FURTHER READING

Numerous books are available on cacti and succulents. Some deal with only a single genus or family, while others treat entire groups or growth forms. Still others provide a treatment of regions that are rich in succulents. Arguably the best-advanced, although rather technical, series on the taxonomy of succulents of the world is the multi-volume *Illustrated Handbook of Succulents*, variously edited by U. Eggli and H.E.K. Hartmann and published by Springer-Verlag.

The following is a small selection of books that can be consulted on cacti and succulents:

Anderson, E. F. 2001. *The cactus family*. Timber Press, Portland.

Anderson, M. 1998. *The ultimate book of cacti and succulents*. Lorenz Books, New York.

Baldwin, D. L. 2007. *Designing with succulents*. Timber Press, Portland.

Baldwin, D. L. 2010. *Succulent container gardens*. Timber Press, Portland.

Baldwin, D. L. 2013. *Succulents simplified*. Timber Press, Portland.

Benadom, D. 2013. *Superb succulents*. A selection (predominantly) of winning plants from succulent shows that have been potted and staged for perfection. Superb Succulents, Simi Valley.

Benadom, D. 2014. *Echinocereus*. Decades of field experience, photography, and dedication to a phenomenal genus of cacti. Superb Succulents, Simi Valley, California.

Benadom, D. 2015. *Southwest Deserts*. California & Nevada. Superb Succulents, Simi Valley, California.

Charles, G. 2003. *Cacti and succulents*. An illustrated guide to the plants and their cultivation. Crowood Press, Ramsbury.

Cullmann, W., Götz, E, & Gröner, G. 1986. *The encyclopedia of cacti*. Alphabooks, Sherborne.

Eggli, U. (Editor) 2001. *Illustrated handbook of succulents plants*. (Various volumes). Springer Verlag, Berlin.

Grantham, K. & Klaassen, P. 1999. T*he plantfinder's guide to cacti & other succulents*. David & Charles Publishers, Newton Abbot.

Hewitt, T. 1993. *The complete book of cacti & succulents*. Dorling Kindersley. London.

Hunt, D. (comp.) 1999. *CITES Cactaceae checklist*. 2nd edn. Royal Botanic Gardens Kew & International Organization for Succulent Plant Study, Richmond & Zürich.

Hunt, D., Taylor, N. & CHARLES, G. (Editors). 2006a. *The new cactus lexicon*. Text. dh books, Milborne Port, England.

Hunt, D., Taylor, N. & CHARLES, G. (Editors). 2006b. *The new cactus lexicon*. Atlas of illustrations. dh books, Milborne Port, England.

Mace, T. & Mace, S. 1998. *Cactus and succulents*. A Hamlyn care manual. Hamlyn, London.

Moore, J. 2014. *Under the spell of succulents*. A sampler of the diversity of succulents in cultivation. Jeff Moore, Solana Succulents, place of publication not stated.

Moore, J. 2016. *Aloes and agaves in cultivation*. Jeff Moore, Solana Succulents, place of publication not stated.

Smith, G. F. 2003. *First field guide to the aloes of southern Africa*. Struik, Cape Town.

Smith, G. F., Van Jaarsveld, E.J., Arnold, T. H., Steffens, F. E., Dixon, R. D. & Retief, J. A. 1997. *List of southern African succulent plants*. Umdaus Press, Pretoria.

Smith, G. F. & VAN WYK, B. [A.E.]. 2008. *Aloes in southern Africa*. Struik Publishers, Cape Town.

Smith, G. F. 2005. *Gardening with succulents*. Horticultural gifts from extreme environments and the arid world. Struik Publishers, Cape Town.

Smith, G. F., Chesselet, P., Van Jaarsveld, E., Hartmann, H., Hammer, S., Van Wyk, B-E., Burgoyne, P., Klak, C. & Kurzweil, H. 1998. *Mesembs of the world*. Briza Publications, Pretoria.

Smith, G. F. & Crouch, N.R. 2009. *Guide to succulents of Southern Africa*. Struik Nature, Cape Town.

Smith, G. F., Crouch, N.R. & FIGUEIREDO, E. 2017. *Field guide to succulents in Southern Africa*. Struik Nature, Cape Town.

Smith, G. F. & Figueiredo, E. 2013. *Succulent paradise*. Twelve great gardens of the world. Struik Lifestyle, Cape Town.

Van Jaarsveld, E. J., Van Wyk, B-E. & Smith, G. F. 2000. *Succulents of South Africa*. A guide to the regional diversity. Tafelberg Publishers, Cape Town.

Van Wyk, A.E. & Smith, G. F. 2001. *Regions of floristic endemism in southern Africa*. A review with emphasis on succulents. Umdaus Press, Hatfield.

Van Wyk, B.E. & Smith, G. F. 2014. *Guide to the aloes of South Africa*. 3rd edition. Briza Publications, Pretoria.

CREDITS

WEBSITES

Many cacti and succulent organizations and societies manage sites dedicated to some or all of the plant groups that include cacti and succulents. The most useful website for information on cacti is undoubtedly http://www.cactus-mall.com. Many global societies have links to this site and it is well worth a visit. A selection of other websites includes:

www.cssainc.org

www.gasteria.org

www.desertmuseum.org

www.kaktus.dk

www.columnar-cacti.org

www.lithops.net

www.desert-tropicals.com/plant

www.mammillaria.net

www.hawothia.com

www.cactusexpeditions.com.ar

Photographic credits

All photography by Gideon F. Smith except as noted here: (Shutterstock: cover: John_T, spine: Maleo, page 105: eFesenko); (Adobe Stock: back cover: eqroy, page ii: Mara Zemgaliete, pages 6 & 7: zeakauri, pages 8 & 9: laura, pages 36 & 37: wareelak).